Herbs
in Healthy Home Cooking

JESSICA HOUDRET

Herbs
in Healthy Home Cooking

ASHGROVE PRESS, BATH

First published in Great Britain by
ASHGROVE PRESS LIMITED
4 Brassmill Centre, Brassmill Lane, Bath, Avon BA1 3JN

© Jessica Houdret 1993

ISBN 1 85398 037 4

First published 1992
Photoset in 10/11½ Palatino by
Ann Buchan (Typesetters), Middlesex
Printed and bound by Dotesios Ltd,
Trowbridge, Wiltshire

CONTENTS

ACKNOWLEDGEMENTS

First, I should like to thank my husband for his patient tasting of all the recipes and constant encouragement in the writing of this book.

My thanks also to Libby Riddell of Cheshire Herbs, and Rosemary Titterington of Iden Croft Herbs for their generous help in providing me with various herbs, out-of-season, for my cooking experiments, for the cover photograph and as specimens for Margaret Whiting's careful and sensitive drawings.

Thanks are also due to my daughters for their recipes and ideas and to my mother for the Spanish Omelette directions.

Part I

Why Use Herbs?

Herbs have been used throughout the ages in cookery to improve the flavour of food, and this is still one of the best reasons for including them in recipes today.

But when it comes to a healthy way of eating, herbs are indispensable. The diet that is 'good for you' becomes good to eat as well. Recent research has established that a diet low in salt, sugar and fat and high in fibre is best for health. Unfortunately it is a way of eating which can be rather bland and boring. This is where herbs come in. Used in the right way, and aided and abetted by a subtle use of spices, herbs can transform a healthy diet into an exciting culinary adventure. In the following pages guidance is given on using twenty-five different herbs in an imaginative way to enliven just such a diet – the kind of diet we all know we really should be eating.

How Herbs Can Help

It is sometimes assumed that a vegetarian diet is automatically a healthy one. But it is perfectly possible to cut out all meat and fish and still be eating far too much fat, salt and sugar.

1 CUTTING DOWN ON FAT

Here a vegetarian has an immediate advantage as a third of total fat intake in the average omniverous diet comes from meat. To make matters worse the fat in meat is mostly highly saturated. But meat is not the only culprit. Full-cream milk and milk products, such as cream and cheese, also contain saturated fats. Then there is all the hidden saturated fat in foods such as pastry, cakes, biscuits, ice-cream, crisps, mayonnaise and chocolate.

Fortunately there are plenty of low-fat dairy products to replace the full-cream ones: skimmed instead of whole milk, yoghurt and fromage frais instead of cream, curd and cottage cheeses instead of Stilton, Cheddar, Parmesan and other hard cheeses. Edam has one of the lowest fat contents of the hard cheeses and there is an extra low-fat version as well. Low-fat Cheddar type cheeses are also available. A wide variety of vegetarian cheeses, free from animal rennet, is available from specialist shops and now from some of the large supermarket chains. Look out for the Vegetarian Society V symbol on packaging. A list of suppliers of vegetarian cheeses can be obtained by sending a stamped addressed envelope to: The Vegetarian Society, Parkdale, Dunham Road, Altrincham, Cheshire WA14 4QG.

The distinction between saturated and unsaturated fats is important.

The evidence from the many research studies undertaken over the past decade is that too much saturated fat in the diet raises cholesterol in the blood to unacceptable levels, leading to heart disease and other disorders; whereas unsaturated fats (polyunsaturates and monounsaturates) are not harmful to health. Some studies have shown that they actually contribute to lowering blood cholesterol levels.

The consensus of opinion, however, is that all fats should be restricted to some extent, though unsaturated fats should be eaten in preference to saturated where possible.

Saturated fats are animal fats, butter, cream, some margarines and vegetable cooking fats, also palm oil and coconut oil.

Polyunsaturated fats include oils such as sunflower, safflower, corn and soya and certain vegetable margarines (labelled 'high in polyunsaturates').

Monounsaturated fats, so named because of their different chemical structure, are just as acceptable from a health point of view. Olive oil comes into this category.

Although nuts have a high fat content, it is of the healthful, polyunsaturated variety and as they contain other valuable nutrients as well, they make a useful addition to the vegetarian diet. But ready-roasted and salted snack nuts, which are often cooked with additional oil, should be avoided.

Egg yolks contain both fat and cholesterol (the whites have none). But cholesterol in itself is not harmful. In fact it is essential for the healthy functioning of the nervous system. It is only when a build-up occurs, from eating too much saturated fat, that it becomes dangerous. If you are already eating quantities of meat, butter and cream – too many eggs as well would obviously be an overload. But in a healthy, high-fibre, low-in-saturated-fat vegetarian diet, a few eggs would not be out of place.

As with most things, moderation is the key-word.

Herbs counteract the blandness of low-fat dishes.

2   EATING LESS SUGAR

This means cutting down, of course, on sweets, cakes, jams and jellies, shop-bought fruit yoghurts and desserts. But don't forget all the hidden sugar in chutneys, tomato ketchup, baked beans, cereals, soft drinks, most tinned foods and indeed alcohol.

Extra sugar is not necessary at all in the diet, but to cut it out completely seems unrealistic.

Herbs can be used to flavour sugar-free chutneys and sauces and some, such as angelica and sweet cicely, act as sweeteners by reducing the acidity of fruit with a tart taste.

3 EATING LESS SALT

Salt is an excellent preservative and is present in quite large quantities in processed, canned and packeted foods. Try adding salt with a very light touch to your cooking and don't add extra at the table.

A certain amount of salt is necessary in the diet, but experts are agreed that too much does not lead to good health and increases, amongst other things, the likelihood of high blood pressure.

Herbs, especially the stronger-tasting ones, and herb seasonings make it possible to cut down on salt.

4 EATING MORE FIBRE

Fibre is the structural part of vegetables, fruit and cereals; the part that holds them together, so to speak. It does not contain nourishment in itself but is vital to a healthy digestive process.

It is present in:

a) All fruits and vegetables.

b) Pulses – that is dried peas and beans, lentils etc.

c) Whole cereals – that is whole wheat, oatmeal and brown rice.

Bran is the fibrous part of whole wheat and is extracted during the milling and refining process to produce white flour. There is no need, therefore, to add extra bran to food if your diet contains an adequate proportion of high-fibre foods.

Herbs add interest to dishes made with high-fibre ingredients.

Fresh or Dry?

Most herbs are nicest fresh. But there are a number which retain a good flavour when dried, though the only one I would recommend using dried for preference is bay.

Some herbs are evergreen – rosemary, winter savory, thyme and sage for instance. But their concentration of essential oils is not as strong during the winter months, nor is it always advisable to pick too much from the plant out of the growing season when it is not renewing itself.

Many die back in the winter, or are annuals. It is essential, then, to have a stock of dried herbs for the months when fresh herbs are out of season.

There are many brands of dried herb on the market but if you dry your own you can be sure they are of good quality, not stale or contaminated, and, if you follow a few simple guidelines, they will have a better flavour and colour than most you can buy. (See pages 20–44) Guidance on the drying propensities of individual herbs is given under their listing in THE HERBS IN DETAIL (pages 20–44).

Dried herbs have a more concentrated flavour than fresh ones, as they have had the water content extracted. A general rule-of-thumb is that you need one third the amount of a dried herb that you would of a fresh herb, i.e. 1 teaspoon dried herb = 3 teaspoons fresh herb.

TO DRY HERBS

This is still the best way of preserving herbs.

To harvest   –   for maximum flavour herbs should be harvested just before they come into flower. Pick them on a dry day, preferably in the morning, after the dew has evaporated but before the sun has drawn out too much of the essential oil content.

To dry   –   Tie them with raffia, or string, in small bunches and hang to dry in a warm, airy place out of direct light. When the leaves are crackly and paper-dry to the touch (about one week to ten days depending on the thickness of the leaf) they may be stripped from their stalks and stored. (This method is suitable for

15

BAY, HYSSOP LEAVES, MINT, ROSEMARY, SAGE, SAVORY, THYME).
Alternatively, strip the leaves, or petals before they are dried.
Then spread them in small, slatted fruit crates (obtainable from
supermarkets), lined with tissue paper, and stacked one on top of
the other in a warm airing-cupboard. Leave them for about one
week, until they are crackly and paper-dry to the touch. (This
method is suitable for CHERVIL, MARJORAM, PARSLEY, FRENCH
TARRAGON, LOVAGE, HYSSOP FLOWERS, POT MARIGOLD PETALS).
    To dry the seeds of FENNEL, DILL, CORIANDER, tie in bunches with
the seed-heads suspended in paper bags. When dry, the seeds will
fall away from the husks.
    To dry ORANGE and LEMON PEEL for use in herb seasonings, pare
rind off finely, without any pith, using a potato peeler. Cut the
rind into small pieces and dry in a warm airing-cupboard for two
to three weeks, or in a very low oven for several hours, or in a
microwave oven for 5–6 minutes. Once the peel is hard pulverise it
in a mortar until reduced to a finely crumbled consistency, before
adding to seasonings.

DRYING HERBS IN A MICROWAVE OVEN

Conventional domestic ovens are not suitable for drying herbs,
but successful results can be obtained from a microwave oven,
because of the lack of surface heat and the very short processing
time involved.
    The snag is that it is fiddly and time-consuming to dry herbs in
any quantity. Only limited amounts can be placed on the turntable
at one time and quite large bunches of fresh herbs are needed to
produce a significant amount when dried.

To dry   – place small bunches of herbs on kitchen paper in the
microwave oven and process for 2–3 minutes, depending on the
thickness of the leaf and moisture content of the herb.

TO FREEZE HERBS

Freezing them is another way to preserve some herbs. They will
not be suitable for use as a garnish once defrosted and do not have
a very long storage life – two or three months as opposed to the
year for which dried herbs remain potent.

To freeze — simply put small bunches into cellophane bags, or well-scoured empty margarine or yoghurt tubs, and put in the freezer. BASIL, CHERVIL, CHIVES, PARSLEY, TARRAGON, SORREL, MARJORAM and SAVORY can all be frozen with some success.

Herbs can also be frozen chopped, either in single varieties, or in combinations such as *fines herbes*.

Herbs for inclusion in soups and stews can be frozen in ice-cubes, which can then be stirred in whole during the cooking process.

Which Herbs?

Listed below are twenty-five herbs which will add an extra dimension to the repertoire of the health-conscious cook.

* All 25 will enhance a low-fat, high-fibre diet.
* 12–20 are helpful when reducing salt in the diet.
* 21–25 are suitable for use in sweet dishes and for cutting back on sugar.
* 11 – Rosemary – fits all three categories.

You may not be used to some of the herbs, such as hyssop, as a culinary herb. Some you may be more familiar with in their role as garden flowers. You don't need to use them all of course; just try them out gradually as they appeal to you.

1 BAY (*Laurus nobilis*)
2 BASIL (*Ocimum basilicum*)
3 CHERVIL (*Anthriscus cerefolium*)
4 CHIVES (*Allium schoenoprasum*)
5 PARSLEY (*Petroselinum crispum*)
6 TARRAGON (*Artemisia dracunculus*)
7 FENNEL (*Foeniculum vulgare*)
8 DILL (*Anethum graveolens*)
9 SORREL (*Rumex acetosa*)
10 POT MARIGOLD (*Calendula officinalis*)
11 ROSEMARY (*Rosmarinus officinalis*)
12 MARJORAM – Knotted or Sweet Marjoram (*Oreganum majorana*)
      Pot Marjoram (*O. Onites*)
      Wild Marjoram or Oregano (*O. vulgare*)
13 SAVORY – Summer Savory (*Satureja hortensis*)
      Winter Savory (*S. montana*)
14 SAGE (*Salvia officinalis*)
15 THYME (*Thymus vulgaris*)
16 LOVAGE (*Levisticum officinale*)
17 BORAGE (*Borago officinalis*)
18 CORIANDER (*Coriandrum sativum*)
19 HYSSOP (*Hyssopus officinalis*)

20 NASTURTIUM (*Tropaeolum majus*)
21 ANGELICA (*Angelica archangelica*)
22 SWEET CICELY (*Myrrhis odorata*)
23 MINT – Spearmint (*Mentha spicata*)
         Applemint (*M. rotundifolia*)
         Peppermint (*M. piperita*)
24 LEMON BALM (*Melissa officinalis*)
25 ROSE (*Rosa gallica officinalis*)

GARLIC

Although often categorised as a herb, and certainly indispensable to the health-conscious cook, garlic is not included in the above lists. For these purposes it is considered to be in the same category as onions and its inclusion in recipes is taken for granted.

The Herbs in Detail

In this section you will find the general uses of each herb and whether they are best used fresh or dry. If you are going to use herbs in cooking to any extent you will probably want to grow some for yourself, so hints on cultivation are also included. If you have no garden, many can be successfully raised on the kitchen windowsill.

1   BAY (*Laurus nobilis*)

How to Use   In soups, vegetable casseroles, marinades; can be added to the water when cooking dried fruit, potatoes, parsnips, artichokes; use to flavour sauces and milk puddings; makes a pretty garnish (fresh) for sorbets and desserts; a principle component of bouquet garni.

Fresh or Dry?   Can be used fresh or dry – but for most purposes dried leaves are best as the flavour is more potent.

To Grow   Bay is an evergreen shrub, or tree, native to the Mediterranean region and, if grown outside, should be planted in a sheltered position, as it is susceptible to frost damage. A good solution is to grow it in a large tub so that it can stand outside in the summer and be brought indoors for the winter.

2   BASIL (*Ocimum basilicum*)

Also known as sweet basil, this is the one with the best flavour. But the purple variety (*O. basilicum purpurascens*) and bush or dwarf basil (*O. minimum*) can also be used in cooking.

How to Use   In pizzas and pasta dishes; with baked eggs; in herb oils and vinegars; in herb cheeses and dips; snipped into salads; has a special affinity with tomatoes and aubergines.

Fresh or Dry?   The fresh leaves are by far the best as basil does not dry well. Can be frozen with reasonable success.

To Grow Outdoors   Native to India and widely grown in Mediterranean countries, basil is classed as a half-hardy annual in this country. Grow it from seed, sown under glass in April or May, transplanting the seedlings to their final position when danger of frost is past. For best results grow in a large pot, on the patio, keeping well watered.

Indoors   Grows well in a pot on the windowsill.

3   CHERVIL (*Anthriscus cerefolium*)

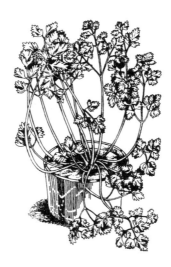

Looks a little like parsley, but has a delicate flavour all of its own. Brings out the flavour of other herbs. Always add to recipes at the last minute as it loses flavour if overcooked.

How to Use   With rice; in egg dishes; in herb cheeses and dips; in vegetable dishes; stir into mashed potato; add to herb seasonings; an ingredient of *fines herbes*.

Fresh or Dry?   Fresh – the leaves lose flavour if dried but are still worth including in dried herb seasonings.

To Grow Outdoors   A hardy annual; sow where it is to grow as it prefers not to be transplanted. Successional sowing will ensure a continuous supply throughout the summer. Water well so that it does not run to seed too quickly.

Indoors   Grows well in a window-box or in a seed-tray on the windowsill.

4 CHIVES (*Allium schoenoprasum*)

For a change, try garlic chives (*A. tuberosum*), an interesting variety with a pronounced garlicky tang.

How to Use   Add to herb cheeses and dips; savoury mousses; quiches; salads and salad dressings; omelettes; as a garnish for soups (chives is the traditional garnish for the chilled leek and potato soup, vichyssoise); component of *fines herbes*.

Fresh or Dry?   Chives do not dry well but *can* be frozen. To freeze, snip into a small polythene bag or empty margarine tub. They are best fresh.

To Grow Outdoors   Slow to establish from seed; for quickest results buy a clump, then divide in the autumn or spring every two years and you will soon have plenty. To ensure a continuous supply of leaves, cut off the flower heads as soon as they appear.

Indoors   Can be grown most successfully in a windowsill pot.

5 PARSLEY (*Petroselinum crispum*)

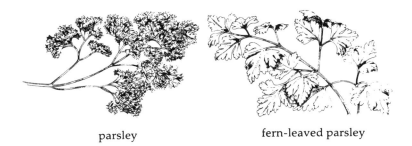

parsley   fern-leaved parsley

Fern-leaved or French parsley is also worth growing and has a better flavour. Parsley is an excellent source of iron and vitamins A and C. Probably the herb with the widest culinary use.

How to Use Snip into salads, salad dressings, baked eggs, scrambled eggs, omelettes; add to savoury stuffings and dumplings; use the stalks to flavour soups and vegetable casseroles, with the snipped leaves as garnish; component of bouquet garni; add to herb cheeses and butters; marinades; savoury mousses, quiches; snip over cooked vegetables; component of *fines herbes*.

Fresh or Dry? The leaves are not worth drying except to add balance to a herb seasoning. Parsley can be frozen, in plastic bags or ice-cubes, for inclusion in cooked dishes. It will be too limp when thawed to use as a garnish.

To Grow Outdoors Parsley is a biennial, but is best treated as an annual. Grow from seed each year. For ease of germination sow in a seed-box in gentle heat, then transplant seedlings carefully to outdoor position. Grow in rich soil and keep well watered. If conditions are favourable it will self-seed.

Indoors Can be grown successfully in windowsill pot or window-box.

6   TARRAGON (*Artemisia dracunculus*)

It is important to make sure you have French tarragon, not the inferior, stronger-growing Russian variety, which is tasteless. Test by picking off a leaf and rolling it between the fingers to release the unmistakable, sweetish scent. Russian tarragon is virtually odourless.

How to Use   With dried peas and beans, sauces and egg dishes; sprinkled over steamed vegetables; it has an affinity with carrots, emphasising their sweetness; add to herb oils and vinegars; salad dressings; component of *fines herbes*.

Fresh or Dry?   Although nicest fresh, it retains a reasonably good flavour when dried.

To Grow Outdoors   It *must* be grown from cuttings, or by dividing the underground runners in spring, as true French tarragon does not set seed. Seed packets will contain the Russian kind. Grow in a light, dry soil and give some protection in severe weather.

Indoors   Does not flourish indoors, but can be grown on a sunny patio in a large, well-drained pot.

7   FENNEL (*Foeniculum vulgare*)

Both the leaves and the seeds are used. Florence fennel (*F. dulce*) is the one with the bulbous stem. Both have an aniseed flavour.

How to Use   LEAVES – in salads and vegetable dishes; with pasta. SEEDS – in stir-fry dishes; vegetable casseroles; in pickles and marinades.
BULBOUS STEM of Florence fennel can be shredded raw in salads; braised as a vegetable.
WOODY STEMS of *F. vulgare*. Cut them down at the end of the growing season and use as an aromatic fuel for the barbecue when grilling fish.

Fresh or Dry?   The leaves are best fresh.

To Grow Outdoors   A perennial, fennel is a large plant which needs room. It is easy to grow from seed and prefers a sunny position and well-drained soil. Self-seeds.

Indoors   Not suitable to grow indoors.

8   DILL (*Anethum graveolens*)

Both seeds and leaves are used. The leaves are sometimes called 'dillweed'. It is much used in Scandinavian cookery.

How to Use   LEAVES – in vegetable dishes; in salads and salad dressings; sauces; herb vinegar; in dips and herb cheeses; has an affinity with cucumber and courgettes.
SEEDS – in stir-fry and vegetable dishes; in marinades, herb vinegar and pickles.

Fresh or Dry?   The leaves are best fresh, losing most of their flavour when dried. The dried seeds, of course, retain a good flavour.

To Grow Outdoors   An annual, dill is best sown where it is to be grown, as it does not take well to being transplanted. Sow successively for a good supply throughout the summer, thinning out to 8 ins. (20 cm) apart.

Indoors   Can be grown on the windowsill. Sow a few seeds in a good-sized pot, then thin out to leave 3 or 4 plants.

9   SORREL (*Rumex acetosa*)

This is the ordinary garden sorrel. French sorrel (*R. scutatus*) has smaller, arrow-shaped leaves; it also has a better flavour. The taste is refreshing, sharp and lemony. Sorrel is rich in vitamin C and considered to have blood-cleansing properties. It is also high in oxalic acid and should be eaten sparingly if one is prone to rheumatism.

How to Use   To make soup; in vegetable or egg mousses; in omelettes; as fritters; with spinach; in white sauce; in savoury stuffed pancakes.

Fresh or Dry?   The leaves should be used fresh when young. They cannot be dried for use in cookery, but freeze successfully.

To Grow Outdoors   A perennial, grow from seed sown in spring in damp, rich soil. Keep well watered. French sorrel will tolerate drier conditions than garden sorrel.

Indoors   Not suitable as a windowsill plant.

10   POT MARIGOLD (*Calendula officinalis*)

Not often thought of nowadays as a culinary herb, but it adds colour and interest to a wide variety of dishes. The bright orange petals are the part to use. (Do *not* use French or African marigolds (*Tagetes*) for culinary purposes!)

How to Use   Add to rice dishes; sprinkle over salads and desserts; pound in a mortar and add to low-fat cheeses; add to biscuits, scones or herb bread.

Fresh or Dry?   Use fresh in season. The petals also dry well. Store in an opaque container to retain maximum colour.

To Grow Outdoors   An easy-to-grow annual. Sow in spring, where they are to grow, for a summer-long supply. Self-seeds.

Indoors   A good subject for a window-box or patio tub – make sure they have plenty of light.

11   ROSEMARY (*Rosmarinus officinalis*)

A deliciously aromatic herb which can be used in both sweet and savoury dishes – but with discretion as the flavour is strong.

How to Use   In vegetable hot-pots; chestnut loaf; rosemary jelly; to flavour oil and vinegar; with baked apples; in fruit pies and flans; in biscuits or scones; flowers can be crystallised or used to flavour sugar for desserts or as a garnish for fruit salads.

Fresh or Dry?   The fresh leaves are preferable. Although the dried leaves retain a good flavour, they become rather brittle and spikey.

To Grow Outdoors   Of Mediterranean origin, rosemary should be grown in a sheltered south-facing position. It prefers a light, well-drained soil. Propagate from cuttings and protect from frost until well established.

Indoors   Can be grown indoors in a large well-drained pot.

Salt Restriction

Although they have many other uses in cooking, the following nine herbs (12–20) are especially useful in a diet where salt is restricted.

12 MARJORAM (*Oreganum*)

sweet marjoram

perennial marjoram

A warm, spicy herb. Sweet or knotted marjoram (*Oreganum majorana*) is an annual and has, perhaps, the best flavour. The perennial marjoram (*O. onites*) is also good for culinary purposes. Wild marjoram, or oregano (*O. vulgare*) has a stronger flavour when grown in a hot, dry climate.

How to Use Popular in Mediterranean cookery; use in pasta dishes and pizzas; with pulses; in vegetable soups and stews; with cooked vegetables – it goes especially well with potatoes, either mashed, sautéed or scalloped. Often added to bouquet garni along with bay, parsley and thyme; in herb seasonings.

Fresh or Dry? Best fresh but retains quite a good flavour when dried.

To Grow Outdoors Grow the annual sweet majoram from seed. Pot marjoram, which is hardy, should be propagated by root division or cuttings, as should wild marjoram or oregano. A sunny, sheltered position is best and reasonably rich soil.

Indoors Can be grown in a pot on the windowsill, but is inclined to get 'leggy'.

13 SAVORY *(Satureja)*

Summer savory   Winter savory

Summer savory *(Satureja hortensis)* is the annual variety. Winter savory *(S. montana)* is a perennial and evergreen. They both have a strong, spicy taste, but summer savory has the edge when it comes to the best flavour.

How to Use In vegetable and pulse dishes – has a special affinity with beans; soups, terrines and quiches; herb seasonings.

Fresh or Dry? Best when fresh, but the flavour is reasonably good when dried. Grow both varieties for a year-round supply.

To Grow Outdoors Grow summer savory from seed. As the seedlings are tiny, for best results, start them off in a seedbox, transplanting when they have made some growth and are stronger. Grow winter savory from cuttings or propagate by root division.

Indoors Winter savory is the best one to grow in a windowsill pot.

14 SAGE (*Salvia officinalis*)

The purple variety (*S. purpurascens*) makes a colourful alternative. Sage is strong tasting, so add it sparingly.

How to Use   In pasta and pulse dishes; in nut loaf or burgers; in herb cheeses and herb seasonings.

Fresh or Dry?   As it does not lose its leaves in winter, sage can be used fresh for most of the year. But the leaves do dry well and retain a good flavour.

To Grow Outdoors   Best grown from cuttings. A hardy perennial, plants should be renewed every four or five years as they become 'leggy' and 'woody'.

Indoors   Can be grown on a windowsill – but needs a large pot.

15   THYME (*Thymus vulgaris*)

Lemon thyme (*T. citriodorus*) and golden lemon thyme (*T. citriodorus aureus*) are other varieties to try.

How to Use   In soups, and vegetable casseroles; with pulses; in marinades; in scones and herb bread; in herb seasonings; component of bouquet garni.

Fresh or Dry?   Equally good fresh or dry.

To Grow Outdoors   A perennial of the Mediterranean region, it grows best in well-drained, fairly poor soil. Easy to propagate, it can be grown from seed, cuttings or division of roots.

Indoors   Thyme can be grown in a windowsill pot. Keep it well trimmed and give adequate water, but do not allow it to become water-logged or to stand with its 'feet' in water.

16 LOVAGE (*Levisticum officinale*)

A useful herb when it comes to cutting back on salt as it has a spicy, celery-like flavour. Use sparingly as the taste is strong. Rich in vitamins.

How to Use In soups and vegetable casseroles; in salads and vegetable dishes; with baked potatoes; pulses; in herb seasonings.

Fresh or Dry? Best used fresh, but a dried supply is useful for the winter and to add to herb seasonings. Can also be frozen.

To Grow Outdoors A perennial which dies back in the winter. Grow from seed, or by root division. It does best in moist, rich soil. Keep well watered in dry weather.

Indoors Not suitable for growing on the windowsill as it is a tall plant reaching 5 ft or more when fully developed.

17   BORAGE (*Borago officinalis*)

It contains a saline mucilage, which makes it useful as a mineral-salt substitute. At the same time it has a refreshing, cucumber flavour, which enhances summer drinks. The dainty, star-shaped flowers can be used to garnish salads and desserts. Borage is rich in potassium and calcium.

How to Use   LEAVES – can be added to soups; when very young, finely chopped in salads; in wine, cider or fruit cups; float a single leaf in a glass of apple juice or mineral water.
FLOWERS – use the fresh flowers as a garnish for salads, desserts and drinks; they can also be crystallized.

Fresh or Dry?   The leaves can be dried for use in a salty herb seasoning.

To Grow Outdoors   An easy-to-grow annual, which self-seeds freely. Borage does best in a sunny position and in well-drained, not-too-rich soil.

Indoors   Not suitable for growing on the windowsill.

18   CORIANDER (*Coriandrum sativum*)

Much used in Eastern cookery and sometimes known as 'Indian parsley'. Both the fresh leaves and the dried seeds are used, the latter sometimes in powdered form. The leaves have a stronger taste than the seeds and should be used sparingly.

How to Use   LEAVES – in curries and rice dishes; with pulses; in stir-fry and vegetable dishes; in salads; as a garnish instead of parsley.
SEEDS – in marinades; curry powder; quiches; vegetable dishes; with dried fruit; in fruit pies and compotes.

Fresh or Dry?   The leaves should be used fresh, and can be found in Asian shops if you don't have your own supply. Buy the dried seeds or, if you grow your own, collect the seeds, when ripe, by cutting, complete with stem, and suspending to dry in small bunches with the seed-heads in a paper-bag. After about 10 days the seeds should fall away from the husks.

To Grow Outside   Coriander is a hardy annual and for best results should be sown thinly where it is to grow, as it does not take very happily to being transplanted. It prefers a light, well-drained soil. Successional sowing is a good idea for a continuing supply.

Indoors Possible to grow on the windowsill, but you will need several plants in a large pot to ensure an adequate supply for culinary use.

19   HYSSOP (*Hyssopus officinalis*)

The leaves are pungent and should be used very sparingly in cooking, but make a valuable addition to herb seasonings for low-salt diets. Hyssop also has glorious blue flowers for sprinkling over salads as a garnish.

How to Use LEAVES – herb seasonings; soups and vegetable casseroles.
FLOWERS – as a garnish for salads.

Fresh or Dry? Use fresh or dry according to season. Both leaves and flowers dry well.

To Grow Outdoors A perennial, easy to grow from seed sown in the spring. As it is not entirely hardy, grow it in a sheltered, sunny position. Light, well-drained soil suits it best. Clip it back in the spring to keep it neat.

Indoors Can be grown in a windowsill pot.

20   NASTURTIUM (*Tropaeolum majus*)

The leaves, seeds and flowers of this familiar garden subject can all be used. The leaves have a strong peppery taste; just a few add distinction to a salad and reduce the need for seasoning. The hot oranges and yellows of the flowers make a spectacular garnish.

How to Use   LEAVES – in salads
FLOWERS – as a garnish for salads and desserts; to flavour vinegar.
SEEDS – pickle as mock capers; to flavour vinegar.

Sugar Restriction

Although some have other uses, the following five herbs help to cut down the amount of sugar added to recipes.

21   ANGELICA (*Angelica archangelica*)

Cook chopped up stems of angelica with rhubarb, or other tart-tasting fruit. It works by counteracting acidity, so that the amount of added sugar can be reduced by half.

How to Use   STEMS, when young and tender – with rhubarb, gooseberries, plums or other sour-tasting fruit; they can also be crystallized.
LEAVES, finely chopped – as a flavouring for savoury soft-cheese dips, or sweet cheesecake.

Fresh or Dry?   Both stems and leaves should be used fresh, but a few leaves can be dried for use in a 'sweet' herb seasoning.

To Grow Outdoors   A large stately plant, angelica is a biennial. It grows best in a damp, well-manured soil in semi-shade, but will tolerate most conditions if it is kept well-watered.

Indoors   Not suitable as a windowsill plant.

22   SWEET CICELY (*Myrrhis odorata*)

A herb which works in the same way as angelica by counteracting the acidity of fruit such as rhubarb. It also has a genuinely sweetish taste of its own, with just a hint of aniseed about it. The leaves are the part to use.

How to Use   With rhubarb, gooseberries, red-currants and black-currants; in summer pudding; in jellies and mousses; fruit salads; in savoury dips and soft cheeses; snipped into salads.

Fresh or Dry?   The leaves should be used fresh. The long seed-pods can be dried for winter use, but they are stronger-tasting and not quite so effective as sweeteners.

To Grow Outdoors   Make sure you buy a plant, or grow it from a reliable seed source, initially, as it is possible to confuse it with cow parsley, or similar wild plants, some of which are poisonous. Sow seed where it is to grow in summer or autumn as it needs first warmth then cold in order to germinate. Seedlings will appear the following spring.

Indoors   Not a suitable subject for the windowsill.

23   MINT (*Mentha*)

The two best varieties for cooking are SPEARMINT (*Mentha spicata*) and APPLEMINT (*M. Rotundifolia*). PEPPERMINT (*M. piperita*) is the one for tea and mint sorbet. Although it has a much wider use in cookery, mint complements sweet dishes and flavours home-made sugarless sauces and chutneys.

How to Use   In fruit salads; sorbets; as a decoration for desserts; in herb jelly; no-sugar chutney; mint sauce; snipped into mixed salads and potato salad; in salad dressings; dips; with cooked vegetables, especially new potatoes and peas; in mint and pea soup; in rice dishes; wholegrain tabbouleh.

Fresh or Dry?   Mint is undoubtedly best fresh, but it's useful to have some dried for winter use.

To Grow Outdoors   Grow from roots or runners in damp, well-manured soil. Mint spreads, so if short of space, confine the roots by burying a bottomless bucket in the soil to surround them, or grow in a large tub by the back door.

Indoors   Can be grown indoors – choose a large pot as the roots need space.

24   LEMON BALM (*Melissa officinalis*)

A herb with a light, lemony taste. It works in the same way as mint, improving sugarless chutneys and low-sugar preserves and adding a subtle flavour to sweet dishes, so making a minimum of sugar necessary.

How to Use   In fruit salads; mousses and jellies; fruit drinks; in chutneys and preserves; salads and salad dressings; in savoury stuffings.

Fresh or Dry?   Should be used fresh, as it loses much of its lovely lemony aroma when dried.

To Grow Outdoors   Very easy to grow from cuttings, root division or seed, and left to itself it will spread rapidly.

Indoors   Can be grown in a pot or window-box. Pinch out the top to encourage bushy growth, keep well watered and make sure the container has good drainage.

25   ROSE (*Rosa gallica officinalis*)

There is a long tradition of using roses in the kitchen and the delicate, scented flavour they give a sweet dish makes too much sugar superfluous. Many varieties are suitable in cookery, apart from the above, the famous 'apothecary's rose', which also has an ancient history as a medicinal herb. Dark crimson 'Ena Harkness' or the bright pink climber, 'Zephirin Drouhin', are two of my favourites.

When using rose petals in cookery, avoid spraying the flowers with chemicals and always cut off the white 'heel' at the base of each petal, which has a bitter taste.

How to Use   In cheesecake; sorbets; mousses; fruit salads; sandwiches; sprinkled over desserts or rice dishes as a garnish; crystallized.

Fresh or Dry?   Use fresh. Dried rose petals are not suitable for culinary use.

Part II

Herbs in Combination

Two classic combinations of herbs from French cuisine, which have stood the test of time, are *fines herbes* and *bouquet garni*. Both have a place in healthy home cooking.

FINES HERBES

Mix together equal quantities of finely chopped PARSLEY, CHIVES, CHERVIL and TARRAGON. *Fines herbes* are best fresh but can also be frozen ready-prepared.

Use: In delicately flavoured dishes which do not require long cooking, such as omelettes and other egg dishes, savoury mousses, herb cheeses and dips, in salads and salad dressings; or sprinkle over hot dishes such as soups and cooked vegetables.

BOUQUET GARNI

This is a little bunch of herbs tied together with string so that it can be easily removed at the end of the cooking process. A BAY LEAF, THYME, PARSLEY or PARSLEY STALKS are always included, other herbs such as a sprig of MARJORAM, SAGE or ROSEMARY are optional.

The same combination of herbs can also be dried, crumbled and put in two teaspoonful amounts into small squares of muslin, gathered into a bundle and tied securely with string.

Use: In dishes requiring longer cooking, such as stocks, soups, vegetable casseroles, also with dried beans, peas and lentils.

HERB SEASONINGS

Ready-made dried herb seasonings are a great convenience. Their addition to recipes will make it unnecessary to add extra salt.

To Make Dry your own herbs if possible, then rub them between the fingers until fine and mix them together following the recipes set out below. You can, of course, experiment and make up your own combinations to suit your taste. (See page 15 for instructions on drying.)

SPICY HERB SEASONING

5 parts dried summer or winter savory
5 parts dried thyme
2 parts dried hyssop
1 part dried orange peel (see page 15)

USE IN: Stuffings, vegetable casseroles, soups, nut loaf, nut burgers, rice dishes, with bean or lentil dishes.

LEMON HERB SEASONING

5 parts dried summer savory
5 parts dried lemon thyme
2 parts dried sage
1 part dried lemon peel (see page 15)

USE IN: Stuffings, soups, wild rice, pasta dishes, with bean or lentil dishes.

SWEET HERB SEASONING

5 parts dried tarragon
5 parts dried chervil
5 parts dried parsley
3 parts dried angelica leaves
2 parts dried marjoram

USE IN: Soups, omelettes and egg dishes, steamed vegetables dishes.

'SALT SUBSTITUTE' HERB SEASONING

5 parts dried lovage leaves
5 parts dried summer savory
2 parts dried parsley
2 parts dried borage

This one is quite strong so add with discretion.

USE IN: Soups, hot-pots, with beans or pulses.

Soups

It's a mystery to me why so few people make their own soups. They are easy to prepare, tasty, nutritious and in every respect superior to the tinned variety.

They can be simple enough for everyday eating, elegant enough for a dinner-party or satisfying enough to provide the basis for a complete meal when served with wholemeal bread, a little cheese perhaps, and followed by fresh fruit.

Fat content is kept to a minimum in the following recipes. Leaving fat out altogether gives just the drab, tasteless results that put people off their good intentions to eat more sensibly. And, in any case, we do need *some* fat in the diet to stay healthy.

Fresh or dry herbs are included according to the appropriate season for the soup, based on availability of ingredients.

If you have not made up batches of the herb seasonings, as suggested, simply use a half-teaspoon of each dried herb mentioned.

The combinations of herbs in these recipes have been carefully chosen to make more than the merest pinch of added salt unnecessary.

The Recipes

		the herbs to include
1	*Vegetable Stock*	– bouquet garni, borage

SPRING AND SUMMER SOUPS

2	*Nettle Soup*	– winter savory, bay leaf
3	*Sorrel Soup*	– sorrel, coriander seeds garnish: snipped chives
4	*Lettuce & Lovage Soup*	– lovage, parsley garnish: snipped parsley
5	*Mint & Pea Soup*	– mint, borage, parsley garnish: whole mint leaves, pot marigold petals
6	*Courgette & Carrot Soup*	– sweet (or green) basil garnish: snipped purple basil

AUTUMN AND WINTER SOUPS

7	*Harvest Festival Soup*	– bouquet garni
8	*Winter Warmer*	– 'salt substitute' herb seasoning (see page 48), bay leaf
9	*Vegetable Velvet*	– bouquet garni, ground coriander
10	*Carrot & Orange Soup*	– 'spicy' herb seasoning, (see page 48), bay leaf garnish: hyssop flowers

Vegetable Stock

1 large onion, peeled
2 sticks celery
2 carrots
1 turnip and/or 1 parsnip
1 tablespoon cider vinegar
2½ pints (1½ *litres*) water
6 peppercorns
½ teaspoon mustard seed
1 teaspoon coriander seeds
2–3 cloves
bouquet garni
3–4 borage leaves
salt to taste

Herbs: bouquet garni, borage

A light vegetable stock will add extra flavour to some of the soups. Alternatively save the water in which greens, or other vegetables, have been cooked. The darker, stronger-tasting stock (directions below) will give some of the winter soups a more full-bodied taste.

It is preferable not to use vegetable stock cubes or concentrates as most are rather salty and overpowering and some contain additives.

Method Cut the vegetables into chunks and crush the spices lightly using pestle and mortar. Then put all the ingredients into a large pan with the water. Cover and bring to the boil. Reduce the heat and simmer gently for 40–45 minutes. Strain the stock before using. It will keep for 3–4 days in a refrigerator and can be frozen.

Dark Stock Fry the vegetables first in a tablespoon of olive oil until lightly brown. Substitute red wine vinegar for cider vinegar and add a teaspoon of soya sauce. Naturally fermented soya sauce, which contains no sugar or additives, (labelled Shoyu) is best if you can get it.

Spring and Summer Soups

Nettle Soup

1 oz (25 g) polyunsaturated
   margarine
1 medium onion, peeled and
   chopped
1 clove garlic, peeled and crushed
1 large potato, peeled and chopped
8 oz (225 g) nettle tops
2 pints (1 litre) vegetable stock or
   water
sprig of winter savory
pinch of mace
1 bay leaf
ground black pepper
pinch of salt OR ½ teaspoon 'salt
   substitute' herb seasoning
¼ pint (150 ml) skimmed milk

Herbs: winter savory, bay leaf

Nettles contain vitamins A and C and are rich in minerals (including calcium, potassium and iron). Traditionally they were eaten in spring for their blood-cleansing properties. They also make a delicious dark-green soup. Pick the nettles when young, taking just the centre leaves from each plant (wearing gloves!). The prickliness will, of course, be lost in the cooking process.

Method   Melt the margarine in a large pan. Add the onion and garlic and cook gently for 3–5 minutes until soft.

Add the potato and 'sweat' over a gentle heat for a further 5 minutes. Add the nettle tops, turning well in the margarine, then add the stock, winter savory, mace, bay leaf, pepper and salt, or 'salt substitute' herb seasoning. Bring to the boil and simmer for 20 minutes. Remove the bay leaf. Liquidise or press through a sieve, then return to the pan and stir in the skimmed milk. Can be served hot or chilled. (Serves 6)

Sorrel Soup

1 oz (25 g) polyunsaturated
   margarine
1 onion, peeled and chopped
1 clove garlic, peeled and crushed
1 teaspoon coriander seeds, crushed
8 oz (225 g) potatoes, peeled and
   diced
8 oz (225 g) sorrel leaves
small bunch purslane leaves
   (optional)
2 pints (1 *litre*) water
freshly grated nutmeg
ground black pepper
pinch of salt (optional)
1 egg yolk
To garnish: a little quark, or fromage
   frais, thinned with skimmed milk,
   and chopped chives.

Herbs: sorrel, coriander seed, chives to garnish

The sharp, lemony flavour of sorrel makes this a most refreshing soup. The addition of purslane, an easy-to-grow, fleshy-leaved annual, counteracts the acidity, but it can be left out if unavailable.

Method Melt the margarine in a pan. Add onion and garlic and cook gently for 5 minutes. Now add the coriander seeds, which you have crushed in a pestle and mortar, then the potato, and cook gently for a further 5 minutes, turning so that it doesn't stick.

Pull the sorrel leaves away from the central spines and add to the pan, along with the water, purslane leaves, nutmeg and seasoning. Bring to the boil and simmer for 20 minutes. Liquidise, then pass through a sieve to remove any trace of stringiness. Return to the pan.

Add a little of the hot liquid to the beaten egg yolk, then stir this into the soup and reheat, being careful not to boil.

Serve garnished with a swirl of thinned quark or fromage frais and snipped chives. Can also be served chilled. (Serves 6)

Lettuce and Lovage Soup

1 oz (25 g) polyunsaturated
margarine
1 large onion, peeled and chopped
2 cloves garlic, peeled and chopped
2 medium potatoes, peeled and diced
2 lettuces, washed and quartered
4–6 lovage leaves
bunch of parsley, tied with string
1 pint (½ *litre*) vegetable stock
1 pint (½ *litre*) skimmed milk
To garnish: yoghurt and snipped
parsley

Herbs: lovage, parsley, snipped parsley to garnish

When all the lettuces in the garden are ready at once, or if you want to use up all those outside leaves, normally discarded, then this is the soup to make. The lovage has a spicy taste, which complements the delicate flavour of the lettuce and makes extra seasoning unnecessary.

This makes a good dinner-party soup, served well chilled and finished with a spiral of yoghurt and finely snipped parsley.

Method Melt the margarine in a large pan, add the onion and garlic and fry, without browning, for 5 minutes, or until tender.

Add the potatoes, lettuce, lovage and parsley and turn well in the margarine, until coated. Add the stock and skimmed milk, bring to the boil and simmer for 20 minutes.

Remove the parsley bunch and liquidise the soup or pass through a sieve. Chill thoroughly and finish with a swirl of yoghurt and snipped parsley. (Serves 6)

Mint and Pea Soup

1 oz (25 g) polyunsaturated margarine
1 small bunch spring onions,
    chopped
1 clove garlic, peeled and crushed
1 lb (450 g) shelled peas
freshly ground black pepper
freshly grated nutmeg
1 pint (½ litre) water
3–4 borage leaves
small bunch parsley, tied with string
1 large bunch spearmint or applemint
    (4–6 stems)
½ pint (300 ml) skimmed milk

Herbs: mint, borage, parsley, whole mint leaves, pot marigold petals to garnish

Make this with fresh peas, if you possibly can, for maximum flavour and a good texture. If you *do* use frozen peas, cut the simmering time down to 10 minutes in all.

Method   Melt the margarine in a pan, add the spring onions and garlic and cook gently for 3 minutes.

Add the peas, black pepper and a good pinch of grated nutmeg and stir over gentle heat for a further 3 minutes.

Add the water, borage leaves and parsley, bring to the boil and simmer for 15 minutes. Then add the mint leaves (stripped from their stalks) and simmer for a further 5 minutes.

Sieve or liquidise the soup in a blender and return to the pan. Add the milk and reheat without boiling.

Serve garnished with whole mint leaves and a scattering of fresh pot marigold petals. (Serves 4)

Courgette and Carrot Soup with Basil

1 tablespoon sunflower oil
1 onion, peeled and chopped
2 cloves garlic, peeled and crushed
1 lb (450 g) courgettes, grated
2 large carrots, grated
1½ pints (850 ml) vegetable stock
freshly ground black pepper
1 dessertspoon chopped sweet basil
To garnish: finely chopped purple basil

Herb: basil (green or 'sweet'), purple basil to garnish

Grated courgettes give this summertime soup its interesting texture, and fresh basil brings out the delicious 'nutty' flavour. It is nicest served hot. Purple basil, if available, makes a pretty contrasting garnish.

Method Heat the oil in a pan, add the onion and garlic and cook gently for 5 minutes until tender but not brown. Then add the grated courgettes and carrots and turn in the oil for 3 minutes.

Add the chicken stock and plenty of ground black pepper. Bring to the boil and simmer for 15 minutes. Add the finely chopped basil and simmer for a further 5 minutes.

Scatter a little chopped purple basil over each serving. (Serves 4)

Autumn and Winter Soups

Harvest Festival Soup

4 small tomatoes
1 tablespoon sunflower oil
1 onion, peeled and chopped
1 small marrow, peeled, de-seeded
   and cut into chunks
2 beetroots, uncooked, peeled and
   chopped
4 carrots, scraped and cut into rings
freshly ground black pepper and
   pinch of salt
freshly grated nutmeg
pinch of mace
2¼ pints (1¼ *litres*) water
bouquet garni
3 tablespoons lentils

Herb: bouquet garni

I always seem to have a glut of marrows and tomatoes in early autumn and devised this recipe to use them up. The addition of carrots and beetroot give it body and a rich, appetising colour.

Method Plunge the tomatoes into boiling water, remove skins and cut into quarters. Heat the oil in a large pan, add the onion and cook until tender (about 5 minutes).

Add marrow, tomatoes, beetroots, carrots, spices and seasoning and turn in the oil until softened (about 5 minutes). Lastly, add the water, bouquet garni and the lentils.

Bring to the boil and simmer for 30 minutes. (OR pressure cook for 8 minutes).

Remove the bouquet garni.

Liquidise the soup in a blender, return to the pan and re-heat before serving. (Serves 6)

Winter Warmer

4 carrots
1 parsnip
1 small turnip
1 medium potato
2 sticks celery
1 tablespoon sunflower oil
1 onion, peeled and chopped
2 cloves garlic, peeled and crushed
1½ pints (*850 ml*) water or dark stock
bay leaf
1 teaspoon 'salt substitute' dried
    herb seasoning (see page 48)
1 wine glass cider

Herbs: 'salt substitute' herb seasoning, bay leaf

No need to liquidise this one, which cuts down on the washing-up! You can vary the veg according to what you have available, and the addition of some ready-cooked kidney or butter beans make it into a satisfying main-course soup.

Method Peel or scrape the vegetables and cut into neat half-inch dice.

Heat the oil in a large pan, add the onion and garlic and fry for 2–3 minutes.

Then add the rest of the vegetables, cover the pan, and leave vegetables to 'sweat' over a very gentle heat for about 10 minutes. Check occasionally that they are not browning too much, and stir to prevent catching.

Lastly, add the water or stock, cider, bay leaf and dried herb seasoning, bring to the boil and simmer for a further 10–15 minutes.

Vegetable Velvet

1 oz (25 g) polyunsaturated margarine
1 medium onion, peeled and
    chopped
2 cloves garlic, peeled and crushed
1 parsnip
3 small or 2 large carrots
1 medium potato
2 sticks celery
1 inch cube fresh ginger, grated
1 teaspoon ground coriander seeds
2 pints (1 *litre*) water
bouquet garni

Herbs: bouquet garni, ground coriander seeds

This is my favourite winter soup – thick and warming, with a subtle hint of ginger. Croutons, made from 1 inch cubes of wholemeal bread, toasted in a medium hot oven until crisp, go well with it.

Method Melt the margarine in a pan and add the onion, and garlic.

Cook over gentle heat until the onion is tender, but not brown (about 5 minutes).

Scrape, or scrub, the other vegetables and cut them up into 1 inch pieces. Add them to the pan with the grated ginger and ground coriander seeds.

Cover the pan and let the vegetables 'sweat' in the margarine for 10–15 minutes, until they are soft and glistening. Be careful that they do not brown or stick. Then add the water and the bouquet garni and simmer for 15 minutes.

Remove the bouquet garni. Liquidise the soup in a blender, or press through a sieve, before serving. (Serves 4)

Carrot and Orange Soup

1 tablespoon sunflower oil
1 large onion, peeled and chopped
1 clove garlic, peeled and crushed
8 oz (*225 g*) carrots
4 oz (*100 g*) split red lentils
1½ pints (*850 ml*) vegetable stock, or water
2 teaspoons spicy herb seasoning, tied into a small square of muslin
1 bay leaf
juice of 2 oranges, grated rind of 1
freshly ground black pepper

Herbs: spicy herb seasoning, (see page 48), bay leaf, hyssop flowers to garnish

This is really a year-round soup, but I find it most appropriate as a bright and cheerful first course for winter entertaining. For a really special finish, scatter dark-blue, dried or fresh hyssop flowers over the soup before serving.

Method   Heat the oil in a pan. Add the onion and garlic and cook gently until soft but not brown – about 5 minutes.

Scrape, then chop the carrots into rings, add them to the pan and turn in the oil for 2 or 3 minutes.

Add the lentils, stock or water, herb seasoning, bay leaf and orange rind. Bring to the boil and simmer for about 25–30 minutes, until the lentils are soft.

Remove the herb seasoning and bay leaf and liquidise or press the soup through a sieve. Return to the pan, add the orange juice and reheat gently.

Serve garnished with a scattering of hyssop flowers. (Serves 4)

Salads

When it comes to salads you can let your imagination take over. Once you have tried a few interesting combinations, you will never be able to look a limp lettuce leaf and statutory wedge of tomato and cucumber in the face again.

There are so many herbs that can be used in a salad you need never serve exactly the same one twice. Basil, chervil, chives, marjoram, mint, parsley, savory, tarragon, coriander, dill, fennel, lemon balm and lovage can all, singly, or in combinations of no more than two (apart from *fines herbes*), be snipped over a basic green salad to give it zest. The flowers of borage, hyssop, nasturtium, pot marigold and rose make delightful garnishes.

But don't overdo it. Herbs should never dominate a salad. They should be no more than a subtle, aromatic suggestion.

The bonus is that you will need a minimum of high-fat salad dressings. Some of the recipes do include a little oil, but a squeeze of lemon juice or dash of herb vinegar is often enough on its own. (See chapter on salad dressings page 70)

The recipes in this section are intended as side salads.

The chapter on Main Dishes (page 91) includes some recipes to serve cold, or as main course salads.

The Recipes

			the herbs to include
1	*Golden Salad Platter*	–	mint, chives, pot marigold petals, nasturtium flowers
2	*Tomato and Mushroom Salad*	–	sweet basil, hyssop flowers
3	*Cucumber Salad with Dill*	–	dill
4	*Royal Purple Salad*	–	purple basil, borage flowers (optional extra – red orache leaves)
5	*Rose Rice Salad*	–	rose petals, chervil
6	*Three-bean Savory Salad*	–	summer or winter savory, parsley stalks, bayleaf
7	*Orange and Chicory Salad*	–	mint
8	*Nasturtium & Beansprout Salad*	–	nasturtium leaves and flowers, mint
9	*Potato Salad with Yoghurt*	–	coriander leaves, chives, ground coriander seeds
10	*Green Salad with Lemon Balm and Lovage*	–	lemon balm, lovage

Golden Salad Platter

lettuce
watercress
Chinese leaves
finely sliced cucumber
very young courgettes, cut into rings
yellow pepper
spring onions
herbs as below

Herbs: mint, chives, pot marigold petals, nasturtium flowers

A spectacular, summer salad which looks good on a buffet table. Vary the salad ingredients according to what is most readily available.

Method On a large serving dish, arrange a selection of green salad vegetables.

De-seed the yellow pepper, cut into thin strips and arrange on top.

Clean the spring onions, leave whole, and place at right angles to the dish, as in the spokes of a wheel.

Snip mint and chives over the salad, finish with a few pot marigold petals and decorate with golden nasturtium flowers.

Tomato and Mushroom Salad

1 lb (450 g) firm tomatoes
4 oz (100 g) mushrooms
2 tablespoons cold-pressed safflower
   or sunflower oil
1 tablespoon fresh basil, finely
   chopped
hyssop flowers to finish

Herb: sweet basil, hyssop flowers

63

Tomatoes and basil are a classic combination and the marriage of flavours is hard to beat. A sprinkling of blue hyssop flowers adds spice and makes a pleasing colour contrast.

Method Using a very sharp knife, cut the tomatoes and mushrooms into wafer-thin slices. Arrange in alternate, overlapping circles on a serving dish. Dribble the oil over the top and finish with the chopped basil and a few hyssop flowers. (Serves 6)

Cucumber Salad with Dill

½ cucumber
1 tablespoon chopped dill leaf
1 tablespoon dill vinegar

Herb: dill

Dill is a delicate herb which complements cucumber and brings out its flavour.

Method Wash the cucumber thoroughly. Score the skin by scraping down it firmly with a fork. Cut into wafer-thin slices. Arrange in a circular pattern on a serving dish and sprinkle with chopped dill and dill vinegar. (Serves 4–6)
(To make dill vinegar, see page 71)

Royal Purple Salad

½ red cabbage
1 bulb Florence fennel, uncooked
5 or 6 sticks of celery
4 oz (*100 g*) black grapes
herbs as below

Herbs: purple basil, borage flowers, optional extra – 5–6 red orache leaves

Basil is known in France as *herbe royale*, which is the inspiration for the name of this salad. Red orache (*Atriplex hortensis rubra*) was planted in medieval monastery gardens. It is a tall thin annual, with a spicy taste, and makes an interesting addition if you have some in the garden. The low-fat salad dressing (page 70) goes well with this.

Method Shred the cabbage, finely slice the Florence fennel, cut the celery into neat pieces and shred any tender young leaves, halve and de-seed grapes.

Arrange salad ingredients on a large platter, sprinkle with finely chopped purple basil and garnish with borage flowers and red orache leaves (if available). (Serves 4–6)

Rose Rice Salad

8 oz (225 g) brown rice
1¼ pints (¾ litre) water
4 oz (100 g) frozen peas
1 medium onion, cut into rings
1 tablespoon sunflower oil
1 hard-boiled egg, roughly chopped
1 tablespoon chervil, chopped
freshly ground black pepper
2–3 tablespoons vinaigrette dressing
2 oz (50 g) sliced, blanched almonds
petals of 1 scented red or pink rose,
    with the white 'heels' snipped off

Herbs: rose petals, chervil

An unusual and decorative salad with a hint of the Middle East. Chervil has a delicate flavour which does not overpower the subtlety of the rose petals.

Method   Put the rice into a pan with the water. Bring to the boil, then cover the pan tightly and simmer for about 20 minutes, until the rice is just tender, adding the peas in the last 5 minutes.

Drain in a colander and rinse in cold water.

Fry the onion rings in the oil until crisp and brown, then mix them into the rice with the chopped chervil and egg. Season with black pepper and moisten with vinaigrette dressing.

Brown the almonds under a grill.

Turn the rice into a serving dish and sprinkle with almonds and rose petals. (Serves 4)

Three-Bean Savory Salad

4 oz (*100 g*) red kidney beans
4 oz (*100 g*) haricot, or butter, beans
8 oz (*225 g*) French or runner beans
1 medium onion, chopped
2 bouquet garnis (made with bay
   leaf, parsley stalks and savory)
3 teaspoons savory, finely chopped
3 teaspoons parsley, finely chopped
1 tablespoon cold-pressed sunflower
   oil
1 tablespoon vinegar
3 teaspoons paprika

Herbs: summer (or winter) savory, parsley stalks, bay leaf

Sometimes known as the 'bean herb', savory goes beautifully with all bean dishes. Read labels carefully if you use tinned kidney and butter beans in this recipe, as most have added sugar and salt.

Method Cook the dried beans separately as follows: Soak overnight. Change the water, bring to the boil and boil vigorously for 10 minutes. Add the bouquet garni and simmer for a further 1 hour, or until tender, topping up water if necessary.

Slice and cook the green beans in a little water until just tender – about 10 minutes. In the last 5 minutes of cooking time, add the chopped onion.

Drain all the beans. Mix together in a serving dish with the savory, parsley, oil and vinegar and paprika. (Serves 6)

Orange and Chicory Salad

4 oranges, peeled and thinly sliced
1 head of chicory, sliced
1 tablespoon mint, finely chopped
A few whole mint leaves

Herb: mint

The sweetness of the oranges sets off the bitter flavour of the chicory, and the mint provides a refreshing tang.

Method Arrange the orange slices on a serving dish, scatter with the chicory and chopped mint. Garnish with the whole mint leaves. (Serves 4–6)

Nasturtium and Beansprout Salad

1 lettuce
6 oz (150 g) beansprouts, blanched for
    2 minutes in boiling water
6–8 nasturtium leaves
6 nasturtium flowers
sprig of mint
2 tablespoons cold-pressed sunflower
    or safflower oil
1 dessertspoon vinegar

Herbs: nasturtium leaves and flowers, mint

Nasturtium leaves are very spicy and compensate for added seasoning. The flowers are edible as well as the leaves, but their primary purpose is decorative.

Method Tear the washed lettuce and nasturtium leaves into shreds. Mix with the drained beansprouts in a salad bowl. Snip the mint into the salad. Just before serving add the oil and vinegar, toss well, then scatter the flowers on top. (Serves 4)

Potato Salad with Yoghurt

1 lb (450 g) new potatoes
4 oz (100 g) plain yoghurt
small bunch fresh coriander leaves
small bunch chives
1 teaspoon ground coriander seeds
freshly ground black pepper
squeeze of lemon juice

Herbs: coriander leaves, chives, ground coriander seeds

Yoghurt makes a delicious low-fat alternative to mayonnaise, or oil-based dressing, in a potato salad.

Method Scrub the potatoes, and cook gently in just boiling water, until tender. Drain, and when cool enough to handle, cut them into cubes and put into a serving bowl.

Chop the herbs finely, beat them into the yoghurt along with the ground coriander, pepper and lemon juice. Mix this into the potatoes while they are still warm, turning till well coated. (Serves 4)

Green Salad with Lemon Balm and Lovage

Herbs: lemon balm, lovage

The fresh taste of lemon balm and spicy taste of lovage combine to give interest to a mixed green salad.

Method Arrange in a large salad bowl a selection of: lettuce leaves; watercress; cucumber, scored and finely sliced; green pepper, de-seeded and sliced; spring onions, finely chopped; avocado, peeled and sliced; mange-tout peas or green beans, lightly cooked and cooled; green broccoli florets.

Snip a small handful of fresh lemon balm leaves and 3–4 lovage leaves over the salad, and sprinkle with lemon juice.

Salad Dressings
Herb Oils and Vinegars

Most traditional salad dressings, unfortunately, have a high fat content. But if you are not eating too much fat in the rest of your diet, there is no harm in bringing out the best in a salad with a little oil and vinegar dressing – 3 parts oil to 1 of vinegar is a good mix, seasoned to taste with salt, pepper and French mustard.

Alternatively try one of the low-fat recipes below or use a sprinkling of herb-flavoured vinegar on its own.

As with everything else do not overdo the herbs – and if you have included fresh herbs in your salad ingredients, keep the dressing plain.

Low-Fat Salad Dressing

2 tablespoons quark or sieved cottage cheese
3 tablespoons yoghurt
1 teaspoon herb vinegar
1 teaspoon paprika

Method Mix all ingredients together. *Fines herbes*, or other chopped herbs of your choice, can be mixed into this dressing if herbs have not already been included in the salad.

Yoghurt Salad Dressing

Thin plain yoghurt with a little skimmed milk. Add a teaspoon of lemon juice and season with freshly ground black pepper, a pinch of garlic salt and, if appropriate, finely chopped fresh herbs as above.

Herb Vinegars

Tarragon, Thyme, Rosemary, Basil, Mint, Marjoram and Savory are all suitable for flavouring vinegar.

Method   Put a good bunch of the chosen herb into a wide-necked jar and bruise the leaves to release the fragrance.

Fill to the top with cider or white wine vinegar. Cover and stand in a warm place, or on a sunny windowsill, for two to three weeks, shaking occasionally, until the flavour of the herbs has permeated the vinegar. For a stronger flavour repeat the process with a fresh bunch of herbs.

Strain the vinegar into clean bottles. A fresh stem of the appropriate herb can be put into each bottle as decoration before sealing with a cork.

For Dill or Fennel Vinegar:
Pick the flower-heads, just before the seeds are ripe. Put them into a jar with some of the leaves of the plant and make as above.

For Nasturtium Vinegar:
Use unripe seeds, flowers and leaves and make as above.

71

Herb Oils

Herb Oils can be used when stir-frying, and in other cooked dishes, as well as for salads and marinades. They are made in much the same way as the vinegars. Use a mild-tasting oil, such as sunflower, and to ensure success sterilise the jar and see that the herbs are scrupulously clean.

Basil, Marjoram, Rosemary, Thyme and Fennel are most suitable for making herb oils.

Method Put a bunch of herbs into a clean jar. Bruise the leaves and cover with oil, making sure the herbs are immersed. Add a teaspoon of cider vinegar. Cover the jar with an airtight lid and leave in a warm (preferably sunny!) place for 2–3 weeks.

Repeat, using fresh herbs.

Strain, pressing the herbs to extract maximum flavour. Pour into sterilised bottles and, for best results, do not replace the discarded herbs with a fresh piece for decoration. Seal with a screw-top, cork or glass stopper and label.

A Word about Oils

Some of the recipes specify 'cold-pressed' vegetable oils. This is because of their superior flavour.

Most vegetable oils on the supermarket shelves are made using a combination of heat and chemical solvents to extract the oil.

Cold-pressed oils, as their name implies, are made by pressing the plant material without the application of external heat, although some heat is generated during this process. Cold-pressed oils are available in health food shops and specialist outlets. Naturally they are more expensive, but it is well worth keeping some for use in salads even if you use a cheaper brand for cooking.

Oils high in polyunsaturated fats are:

sunflower oil
safflower oil
corn oil
sesame oil
soya oil

Olive oil makes an equally healthy choice, even though, containing monounsaturated fats, its chemical structure is different.

Vegetables

If not eaten raw, vegetables are best cooked as briefly and as simply as possible. Steam them in a metal 'flower-petal' steamer or simmer in a very little water. Braising and baking are also good ways to preserve the nutritional value of veg. (Recipes using these methods begin on the opposite page).

Add herbs (with discretion!) instead of salt and pepper or butter. Finely chopped parsley, other single herbs as indicated below, or *fines herbes* can be sprinkled over the cooked vegetables or added at the very end of the cooking time.

The recipes in this section are for vegetables as an accompaniment to the main course. Main course vegetable dishes start on page 91.

Some Special Affinities

Aubergines	– basil
Artichokes	– chervil or bay leaf
Beans – Broad, Runner or French	– summer or winter savory
Beetroots	– mint
Courgettes	– savory, marjoram or basil
Cauliflower	– coriander
Carrots	– tarragon or chervil
Cabbage or Broccoli	– garlic and ginger or juniper berries
Leeks	– lovage
Mushrooms	– marjoram or chives or coriander
Marrow	– parsley or chervil
Parsnips	– rosemary or bay leaf
Potatoes, new, boiled	– mint or chives
baked	– lovage
sauté or scallopped	– marjoram or thyme
Peas, shelled	– mint
mange-tout	– lemon balm
Tomatoes	– basil or marjoram

The Recipes

Baked Aubergines Provençale

2 medium, or 3 small aubergines
4 tomatoes
1 green pepper
1 tablespoon olive oil
2–3 teaspoons finely chopped basil
    (fresh or frozen)
2–3 teaspoons finely chopped parsley

Herbs: basil, parsley

Use the youngest and freshest aubergines you can find – (or, preferably, grow them yourself) – as the skins have a tendency to become bitter and tough with age. If yours *are* of uncertain age, then sprinkle with salt after slicing them, press in a colander for 30 minutes or so, then rinse well and pat dry before using.

Method Cut the aubergines into fairly thin slices, then cut in half again. Skin the tomatoes by plunging first into boiling water, then cut them into thick slices.

De-seed the pepper and cut it into rings, then blanch for 1 minute in boiling water.

Arrange the vegetables in an oven-proof dish, gloss with the olive oil, sprinkle with the basil, cover tightly and bake at 400°C or Gas Mark 6 for 25–30 minutes. Sprinkle with fresh parsley before serving. (Serves 4)

Artichoke Purée

1 lb (450 g) Jerusalem artichokes
2–3 tablespoons skimmed milk
1 bay leaf
twist of black pepper
2–3 teaspoons finely chopped fresh chervil

Herbs: chervil, bay leaf

I find Jerusalem artichokes are much more digestible puréed than whole! They have an interesting and unusual flavour which is complemented by that most subtle of culinary herbs – chervil. The best way to prepare the artichokes is to scrub them with a clean nylon pot-scourer – much easier than trying to peel all those knobbly bits.

Method Scrub the artichokes. Put them in a pan, with the bay leaf, and barely cover with water. Bring to the boil and simmer for about 35 minutes – or until tender. Drain well, remove the bay leaf, add the skimmed milk and pepper then purée in a blender or with a potato masher. Serve sprinkled with finely chopped chervil. (Serves 4)

Boiled Baby Beetroots with Minty Sauce

8–10 small beetroots
5 oz (125 g) plain yoghurt
1 tablespoon finely chopped fresh
OR 2–3 teaspoons dried mint

Herb: spearmint

We are so used to being offered beetroot ready-cooked, cold and often ruined by a soaking in vinegar into the bargain, that it is easy to forget how good it can be as a cooked vegetable. Tiny, young ones are best for this, but, if you are using older beetroots, prepare as below but cook them a little longer and slice before serving.

Method Clean the beetroots, being careful not to damage the skin, then cut off the stalks – leaving about 1 inch (2 *cms*). This is so that they won't bleed during cooking.

Put them into boiling water and cook for about 40–45 minutes, depending on size, until tender.

Drain, allow to cool just sufficiently to handle, then remove the skins and stalks and arrange the beetroots in a serving dish. Put the yoghurt and mint into a saucepan, heat until just below boiling point, pour over the beetroots. (Serves 4)

Savory Courgettes

1 lb (450 g) courgettes
1 clove garlic
1 sprig fresh summer savory (2–3 teaspoons when the leaves are stripped from the stalk)

Herb: summer savory

Method   Wash the courgettes. Do not peel, but slice them fairly thinly. Put them in a steamer (the folding petal type is best for this) over a pan of boiling water, making sure the water level is below the vegetables.

Put the peeled garlic through a garlic-press and sprinkle it over the courgettes with the summer savory.

Cover tightly and steam until tender – about 10–15 minutes. (Serves 4)

Tarragon Baked Carrots

1½ lbs (700 g) carrots
1 scant tablespoon fresh tarragon
OR 2–3 teaspoons dried tarragon
½ oz (25 g) polyunsaturated margarine
twist of freshly-ground black pepper

Herb: tarragon

Tarragon seems to encourage the sweetness of carrots to just the right degree.

As this is one herb which seems to retain its flavour well when dried – especially if you have taken the trouble to dry your own – this way of cooking carrots makes a good year-round stand-by.

Method   Scrub and scrape the carrots and cut them into rings. Put them on a large piece of silver foil on a baking tray. Sprinkle with tarragon and dot with the margarine. Add a twist of black pepper then fold the foil over to form a parcel.

Bake at 400°F, 200°C, Gas Mark 6, for 35–40 minutes until the carrots are tender. (Serves 4)

Marrow Ragoût

1 small marrow
8 oz (225 g) tomatoes
8 oz (225 g) shallots or onions
2–3 cloves garlic
2–3 teaspoons fresh, or frozen, basil
a pinch of cayenne pepper

Herb: basil

A 'ragoût' is traditionally a highly-seasoned dish. In this version basil and a pinch of cayenne pepper provide the right touch. If you have no fresh, or frozen, basil, you could use basil flavoured oil (see page 72) instead.

Method   Using a potato-peeler, peel just the very outside skin from the marrow, so that it is still green. Cut it in half, de-seed and cut into even chunks.

Skin the tomatoes by plunging them first into boiling water, then cut them into quarters.

Peel and chop the shallots or onions, peel and crush the garlic.

Heat the oil in a large pan, lightly cook the onions and garlic first, then add the other vegetables and a pinch of cayenne, cover the pan tightly and cook until everything is tender – 15–20 minutes – adding the basil half-way through the cooking time. (Serves 4–6)

Scalloped Potatoes

1½ lbs (*700 g*) potatoes
1 medium onion, peeled and cut into
    rings
½ pint (*300 ml*) skimmed milk
3 teaspoons fresh, finely chopped
    marjoram OR 1 teaspoon dried
1 teaspoon fresh thyme OR a pinch of
    dried thyme
paprika pepper

Herbs: marjoram, thyme

You can use fresh or dried herbs for this – though, as usual, fresh is best.

It's an ideal way to cook potatoes when you want to put everything into the oven and forget about it.

Method Scrub the potatoes and cut them into thin slices. Layer the slices in an oven-proof dish with the onion rings and herbs. Pour in the milk and sprinkle with paprika. Cover the dish and bake at 375°F, 190°C, Gas Mark 5 for 1–1½ hours – removing the lid for the last 30 minutes to brown the top. (Serves 4)

Steamed Spinach with Sorrel

1 lb (*450 g*) spinach leaves
8 oz (*225 g*) French sorrel
freshly grated nutmeg
½ oz (*25 g*) polyunsaturated
    margarine

Herb: sorrel

Eaten on its own as a vegetable, sorrel can be a little sharp, unless smoothed over with plenty of wicked cream and egg yolks. Try using it, instead, to give a fresh lemon lift to spinach.

Method   Wash the spinach and sorrel leaves well. Put them into a large colander, or vegetable steamer, and stand in a pan of boiling water, making sure that the water level does not reach the vegetables.

Steam for 15 minutes, or until tender but not reduced to rags.

Add the margarine, turning and cutting across with a knife several times until well mixed.

Serve sprinkled with freshly-grated nutmeg. (Serves 4)

Mixed Braised Vegetables

1 head celery
1 small bulb Florence fennel
2 leeks
2 parsnips
2 carrots
1 clove garlic, crushed
1 teaspoon coriander seeds
2 tablespoons sunflower oil
½ pint (*300 ml*) vegetable stock
2–3 sprigs rosemary

Herb: rosemary

The vegetables below make a good combination – but you could use any root vegetables that are available.

Method   Scrub the vegetables well. Slice the fennel in half and then downwards (rather as you would an onion). Discard the outer stems and leaves of the celery and leeks and cut all the vegetables into 2 inch (*5 cm*) pieces.

81

Crush the coriander seeds in a mortar. Heat the oil in a flameproof casserole dish. Add the garlic and coriander seeds and stir them briefly in the sizzling oil, then add the rest of the vegetables, turning them until they glisten.

Pour in the stock, tuck in the rosemary sprigs. Cover tightly and cook in a moderate oven (350°F, 180°C, Gas Mark 4) for about 1 hour, or until the vegetables are tender. (Serves 4–6)

Middle-Eastern Mush-rooms

6 oz (*150 g*) button mushrooms
1 tablespoon sunflower oil
2 tablespoons hummus (buy it ready-made, or make your own see page 144)
2 tablespoons plain yoghurt
1 teaspoon fresh lemon juice
2–3 teaspoons fresh, chopped chives

Herb: chives

Served on toast, this makes a delicious snack or supper dish.

Method Cut the larger mushrooms in half and leave the rest whole. Heat the oil in a small frying-pan. Put in the mushrooms and sauté for 4–5 minutes. Then mix in the hummus, yoghurt and lemon juice, stirring until the sauce bubbles and thickens and the mushrooms are well coated.

Before serving, sprinkle with finely chopped fresh chives.

Starters

Choose from this section when planning a special occasion or three-course meal.

Most of the recipes are also suitable if you want something different for a light, lunch-time dish.

The Recipes

		the herbs to include
1	*Crudités with Fines Herbes Dip*	– Fines Herbes
2	*Sunshine Salad with Lemon Balm*	– salad: lemon balm dressing: chervil or parsley garnish: pot marigold petals
3	*Sorrel Mousse*	– sorrel garnish: fern-leaved parsley
4	*Cucumber Ring*	– chives, parsley, tarragon
5	*Aubergine Terrine* – basil, parsley	– purple basil
6	*Curried Egg Mayonnaise*	– coriander
7	*Jean's Hot Potato Soufflé*	– marjoram

Crudités

Choose from:
carrots
cucumber
cauliflower
purple broccoli
green broccoli
mushrooms
celery
radishes
spring onions
courgettes – very tiny and tender ones
peppers – red, green or yellow
florence fennel
tomatoes

Herbs: For dressing – *fines herbes* (chopped tarragon, chervil, chives and parsley)
For garnish: fern-leaved or French parsley, fennel, pot marigold flowers

One of the simplest, – yet, if decoratively served – most spectacular first courses is a dish of crudités, or sliced, raw, as-fresh-as-possible vegetables, served with a herb dip.

Method Wash vegetables carefully and slice into neat pieces. Divide cauliflower and broccoli into florets, leave radishes whole or cut into 'water-lilies'. Arrange vegetables in rows on a serving dish and serve with a *fines herbes* low-fat salad dressing (see page 70) or herb dip.

For a special occasion presentation, arrange the vegetable pieces, around a central bowl of herb dip, on a raised glass dish. Garnish with sprays of fennel or fern-leaved parsley and small heads of pot marigold flowers.

Sunshine Salad with Lemon Balm

For the salad

½ fresh pineapple, peeled, cored, cut
   into chunks
4 medium carrots, grated
2 oz (50 g) chopped walnuts
2 oz (50 g) sunflower seeds
2 oz (50 g) sultanas or raisins
1 tablespoon lemon juice
1 tablespoon lemon balm leaves,
   finely chopped

For the dressing

4 oz (100 g) plain yoghurt
3 tablespoons sieved cottage cheese
1 dessertspoon parsley or chervil,
   finely chopped

To serve

paprika
lettuce leaves
pot marigold petals (fresh or dry)

Herbs: For the salad – lemon balm
For the dressing – parsley or chervil
For garnish – pot marigold petals

When fresh lemon balm is out of season, add 2–3 teaspoons of home-dried mint to the dressing in addition to the fresh parsley. Lemon balm loses much of its flavour when dried.

Method Mix the dressing ingredients together in a small bowl. Mix all the salad ingredients together, then line individual serving bowls with lettuce leaves and pile salad mixture into each. Top with the dressing and sprinkle with paprika and pot marigold petals. (Serves 6)

Sorrel Mousse

4 oz (*100 g*) sorrel leaves
1 sachet agar-jelly
¼ pint (*150 ml*) vegetable stock
2 tablespoons white wine
4 oz curd cheese
2 egg whites, stiffly beaten
freshly ground black pepper
freshly grated nutmeg
a few sprays of fern-leaved parsley

Herbs: sorrel, fern-leaved parsley

This is a very light dish which makes a good first course.

Method Pull the sorrel leaves away from their central stems. Cook in a very little water for 10 minutes. Drain, and press through a sieve, or blend in a food processor, to make a purée.

Put the agar-jelly into a pan with the cold stock and wine, bring to boiling point while stirring, then add to the purée with the curd cheese. Season with pepper and nutmeg and mix well. Put in a cool place till on the point of setting, then fold in the beaten egg whites. Turn into a mould and chill overnight.

Turn out onto a serving dish, surround with sprays of fern-leaved parsley and triangles of black rye bread. (Serves 6)

Cucumber Ring

1 medium cucumber
12 oz (325 g) curd cheese
4 oz (100 g) quark
3 tablespoons whipping cream
4 spring onions, finely chopped
1 tablespoon each chopped chives,
    parsley and tarragon
freshly ground black pepper

Herbs: chives, parsley, tarragon

The comparatively low-fat content of this pâté is belied by its rich, creamy taste. If you want a really low-fat dish, you could, of course, leave out the cream altogether.

Method Cut 10–12 very fine slices from the cucumber and reserve for garnish. Peel the rest and chop it finely. Put the chopped cucumber in a colander, stand a weighted plate on top and leave for one hour to remove some of the water content. Dry on kitchen paper.

Mix together the curd cheese and quark.

Whisk the cream until floppy, add it to the cheeses with the cucumber, spring onions, chopped herbs and pepper.

Turn into a 1 pint capacity ring mould, put in the refrigerator and leave overnight.

Turn out and serve garnished with cucumber slices. (Serves 6)

Aubergine Terrine

2–3 aubergines (about 1½ lbs [675 g] in all)
2 tomatoes
1 medium onion, peeled and chopped
1 tablespoon lemon juice
2 sprigs fresh basil
2 tablespoons cold-pressed olive oil
1 teaspoon white wine vinegar
1 oz breadcrumbs
salt and freshly ground black pepper
small bunch parsley, finely chopped

Herbs: basil, fresh parsley to garnish

This is based on a popular Greek dish, but the oil content has been considerably reduced. If anything this improves the texture as well as fulfilling health objectives.

Method Bake the aubergines in the oven at 375°F, 190°C, Gas Mark 5, for about 1 hour until soft. Leave to cool, peel, cut in half and discard seeds. Chop up the flesh. Put the tomatoes in a bowl, pour boiling water over them and leave for 5 minutes, then peel, deseed and cut them into chunks.

Liquidise the aubergines, tomatoes, onion, lemon juice and basil to make a paste. Dribble in the olive oil and process again, add the vinegar, seasoning and breadcrumbs.

Spoon into an earthenware terrine dish, or individual ramekins, and garnish with chopped parsley. Chill thoroughly and serve with crusty bread or melba toast. (Serves 4)

Curried Egg 'Mayonn- aise'

6 eggs, hard-boiled
shredded lettuce leaves
1 lemon, cut into 8 wedges

For the mayonnaise sauce
10 oz (250 g) plain yoghurt
2 tablespoons quark
1 tablespoon reduced-calorie
  mayonnaise
1 teaspoon ground coriander
½ teaspoon each ground cumin,
  ground cardamon, turmeric
a pinch of cayenne pepper
3 teaspoons finely chopped coriander
  leaves
a few whole coriander leaves

Herb: coriander – leaves and seeds

The combination of low-fat yoghurt with a little ready-made reduced-calorie mayonnaise makes for a dish much lower in fat than one made entirely with mayonnaise.

Method Cut eggs in half, arrange yolk-side down on a bed of shredded lettuce.

Mix together all the ingredients for the mayonnaise topping until well blended and smooth.

Pour the topping over the eggs and garnish with a few whole coriander leaves and lemon wedges. (Serves 6)

Jean's Hot Potato Soufflé

2 cups mashed potato
2 tablespoons polyunsaturated margarine
2 eggs, separated
1 cup skimmed milk
2–3 teaspoons fresh marjoram, finely chopped OR 1 teaspoon dried marjoram

Herb: marjoram

A hot starter makes a welcome change. This light and airy potato soufflé was often served at Valeswood Herb Farm – run by President of the British Herb Trade Association, Barbara Keen, who has been 50 years in the business. I couldn't resist asking for the recipe.

Method   First prepare the dish. Grease a 1½ pint capacity soufflé dish and tie round it a double band of greased grease-proof paper.

Then beat the margarine and egg yolk into the mashed potato, add the milk and marjoram and mix well. Whisk the egg whites until stiff and fold them into the potato mixture.

Turn into the prepared dish. Stand this in a shallow pan of water and bake in a pre-heated oven, at 400°F, 200°C, Gas Mark 6, for about 30 minutes until well risen and golden-brown. Serve immediately. (Serves 4)

Main Dishes

This chapter is divided into four sections for ease of reference:

* VEGETABLES AND PULSES

* PIZZAS, PASTAS AND PANCAKES

* WHOLE GRAINS, NUTS AND SEEDS

* CHEESE AND EGGS

Vegetables and Pulses

High in fibre, low in fat, rich in variety, vegetables and pulses are central to a healthy diet. Pulses, which include lentils, dried peas and beans, have the added advantage of being a good source of protein for the vegetarian. As pulses can be rather bland in flavour they are greatly improved by the judicious use of herbs.

The Recipes

			the herbs to include
1	*Stuffed Aubergines with Basil*	–	basil
2	*Golden Stuffed Peppers*	–	mint, parsley, 'salt substitute' herb seasoning
• 3	*Savory Beanfeast*	–	summer savory, bay leaf, parsley to garnish
4	*Filled Baked Potatoes*		
	Carrot and Raisin	–	lovage and lemon balm
	Cottage Cheese and Walnut	–	sage and chives
	Tomato and Mushroom	–	coriander
5	*Stir-Fry Vegetables with Fennel*	–	fennel
6	*Winter Casserole*	–	rosemary, thyme
7	*Spiced Lentil Pie*	–	bouquet garni, lovage
8	*Split Pea Slice*	–	bouquet garni, mint, tarragon
9	*Lentil Loaf*	–	bouquet garni, marjoram, savory
10	*Mexican Chilli Bean Stew*	–	coriander

Stuffed Aubergines with Basil

2 large, or 4 small, aubergines
4 oz (100 g) wholemeal breadcrumbs
1 small onion, minced
4 oz (100 g) mushrooms, finely
  chopped
3 teaspoons fresh basil, finely
  chopped
freshly ground black pepper
1 beaten egg

Herb: basil

A particularly filling and tasty main-course vegetarian dish, which has proved popular with even the most dedicated of meat-eaters.

Basil and aubergines go especially well together.

Method Remove the stalks and cut aubergines in half lengthwise. Scoop out the flesh, taking care not to tear the skin. Discard the seeds and chop up the flesh. Put the flesh into a bowl, add breadcrumbs, minced onion, chopped mushrooms basil and pepper.

Mix in the beaten egg. Divide the mixture evenly between the reserved aubergine shells. Wrap in foil, or put in a covered oven-proof dish, and bake at 350°F, 180°C, Gas Mark 4, for 35 mins.

Uncover and continue cooking for 10–15 minutes, until lightly browned. Serve with home-made tomato sauce (see page 146) (Serves 4)

Golden Stuffed Peppers

3 tablespoons sunflower oil
1 onion, peeled and finely chopped
1 clove garlic, peeled and crushed
6 oz (*150 g*) brown rice
1 teaspoon turmeric
1 pint (*600 ml*) water
2 oz (*50 g*) raisins
1 teaspoon 'salt substitute' herb
  seasoning
3 oz (*50 g*) chopped hazelnuts
3 teaspoons finely chopped mint
3 teaspoons finely chopped parsley
4 medium-sized yellow peppers

Herbs: mint, parsley, 'salt substitute' herb seasoning

The flavour in this dish is provided by a combination of dried and fresh herbs. (If you can't get yellow peppers, you could, of course, use green or red ones.)

Method Heat the oil in a saucepan. Add the onion and garlic and fry without browning for 5 minutes. Add the rice and turmeric and fry for a further 2–3 minutes. Add the water, raisins, herb seasoning and bring to the boil, cover the pan tightly, turn down the heat and simmer for 20–25 minutes until the rice is cooked and the water absorbed. Mix in the nuts, mint and parsley.

While the rice is cooking, cut the stalk ends off the peppers, de-seed and core, then blanch them for 3 minutes in boiling water.

Drain well and fill with the rice mixture. Stand the peppers in ¼ pint water (600 ml) (or chicken or vegetable stock) in an ovenproof dish. Bake at 375°F, 190°C or Gas Mark 5, for 35 minutes. (Serves 4)

Savory Beanfeast

1 tablespoon olive oil
1 medium onion, peeled and finely
   chopped
2 cloves garlic, peeled and crushed
1 lb (*450 g*) young broad beans in
   their pods
4 oz (*100 g*) button mushrooms
8 oz (*225 g*) button onions, peeled
   and left whole
1 tablespoon tomato purée
1½ pints (*750 ml*) vegetable stock
1 lb (*450 g*) small new potatoes,
   scrubbed
1 tablespoon fresh summer savory
1 bay leaf
freshly ground black pepper
2 teaspoons paprika
1 tablespoon parsley, finely chopped

Herbs: summer savory, bay leaf, parsley to garnish

This dish was inspired by a simple vegetable stew, prepared in a Greek taverna for the family to eat themselves before they went on their Easter binge. It makes the very best of tender spring vegetables. Young broad beans, in their pods, are simmered with other veg in vegetable stock, spiked with summer savory. If your summer savory is not ready when the broad beans are, use winter savory instead. If you *must* use the dried herb, 1 teaspoon will be enough, but the dish will not have as good a flavour.

Method   Heat the oil in a heavy-bottomed pan. Add the chopped onion and garlic and cook until tender, about 5 mins, stirring intermittently. Cut the bean pods into chunks.

Add the mushrooms, button onions, tomato purée and stock to the pan, then the potatoes, broad beans, summer savory and bay leaf.

Season with black pepper and paprika and simmer for about 15 minutes, or until the beans and potatoes are just tender.

Garnish with chopped parsley and serve piping hot with crusty bread. (Serves 4–6)

Filled
Baked
Potatoes

Baked potatoes, with a variety of fillings, are easy to prepare and make nutritious and versatile main dishes. The addition of strong-tasting, spicy herbs – lovage, coriander and sage – makes extra seasoning unnecessary. Serve with minty yoghurt, instead of butter, and a crunchy salad.

FOR ALL RECIPES

Scrub 4 good-sized potatoes. Bake in a moderately hot oven (400°F, 200°C, Gas Mark 6) until cooked through – about 1 hour. For even results, and to reduce cooking time, spike the potatoes on kebab skewers before putting them in the oven.

When cooked, cut each potato in half, scoop the flesh into a bowl, mash with a little skimmed milk and add filling ingredients of your choice, as given below. Mix thoroughly and pile back into the potato shells. Put them on a baking tray and return to the oven for 15–20 minutes, until heated through and lightly browned.

Top each potato half with a whole leaf of the herb used.

FOR THE FILLINGS:

Carrot and Raisin

4 grated carrots
2 oz (50 g) raisins
4–6 lovage leaves, finely chopped
6–8 lemon balm leaves, finely
    chopped
10 oz (275 g) plain yoghurt
black pepper
1 tablespoon sunflower seeds
1 oz (25 g) shelled pistachio nuts

Herbs: lovage, lemon balm

Method   Mix all the ingredients together, reserving the sunflower seeds to sprinkle on the top of each filled potato half before returning to the oven or grill.

For a quick version, simply split each baked potato almost in half and pile carrot filling in the slit before serving.

Curd Cheese and Walnut

8 oz (225 g) curd cheese
2 oz (50 g) plain low-fat yoghurt
1 tablespoon low-calorie mayonnaise
2 oz (50 g) walnut pieces
3 teaspoons fresh sage, finely
    chopped
small bunch of chives, finely
    chopped

Herbs: sage and chives

Method   Mix all the ingredients together, reserving a few walnuts for decoration.

Tomato and Mushroom

1 oz (25 g) margarine
4 tomatoes, skinned and chopped
   (plunge first into boiling water so
   that skins slip off easily)
2 oz (50 g) mushrooms, sliced
1 medium onion, peeled and chopped
1 clove garlic, peeled and crushed
1 dessertspoon coriander leaves,
   finely chopped
1 teaspoon ground coriander
3 teaspoons paprika

Herb: coriander

Method   Melt the margarine in a pan, then add all the ingredients and cook, stirring, until tender and well blended – about 5 minutes.

(All quantities to serve 4)

Stir-Fry Vegetables with Fennel

2 tablespoons sunflower oil
1 clove garlic, peeled and crushed
1 inch cube of fresh ginger, peeled
   and grated
1 teaspoon fennel seeds
8 oz (225 g) carrots
1 green, or red, pepper, cored and
   de-seeded
small bunch spring onions
4 oz (100 g) mushrooms
3 oz (75 g) beansprouts
2 oz (50 g) blanched, split almonds,
   browned under the grill
2–3 fresh fennel leaves, chopped

Herb: fennel seeds and leaf

Tolerable results can be obtained with a frying-pan, but it is better to use a wok as you can push each cooked batch of vegetables up the sides as you add the next lot, so that nothing becomes overcooked. It is important, too, to start with the veg that takes the longest and finish with the quicker cooking ones, so do keep to the given order.

Method   Wash the vegetables and, except for the beansprouts, cut into fine strips, or small pieces, as appropriate.

Heat the oil in a wok, or large heavy-based frying-pan. Fry the garlic, ginger and fennel seeds for 1 minute, stirring constantly.

Add the vegetables, in the given order, in small batches, frying each batch for 1–2 minutes and stirring all the time.

Finally stir in the almonds, sprinkle with chopped, fresh fennel leaf, and serve immediately, accompanied by plain boiled wholewheat noodles. (Serve 4–6)

Winter Casserole

1 tablespoon olive oil
1 medium onion, peeled and sliced
3 cloves garlic, peeled and crushed
1 teaspoon coriander seeds
2 carrots, cut in rounds
6 oz (*150 g*) swede, diced
2 leeks, sliced
3 sticks celery, sliced
6 oz (*150 g*) button onions, peeled
6 oz (*150 g*) button mushrooms
6 oz (*150 g*) whole chestnuts (canned or frozen)
sprig each of rosemary and thyme
2 bay leaves
1 tablespoon tomato purée
¼ pint (*150 ml*) red wine
¼ pint (*150 ml*) water or vegetable stock

pinch of salt, black pepper, grated
nutmeg
4 potatoes, peeled and sliced
2–3 teaspoons paprika
½ oz (*15 g*) polyunsaturated
margarine

Herbs: rosemary, thyme, bay leaf

The robust flavours of rosemary, thyme and bay leaf give body to this sustaining hot-pot of root vegetables and chestnuts – just right for cold winter days.

For an even lower-fat version, do not fry the onion and vegetables in oil first.

Method Heat the oil in a flame-proof casserole dish. Add the sliced onion and fry for 3–4 minutes. Crush the coriander and add to the pan with the garlic. Stir-fry for a further minute. Put in the vegetables and 'sweat' in the oil for 2–3 minutes. Add the chestnuts, herbs, tomato purée, red wine, water and seasoning.

Arrange the sliced potato on top, dot with margarine and sprinkle with paprika. Transfer to a pre-heated oven (370°F, 190°C, Gas Mark 5) and bake for 50–60 minutes. (Serves 4)

Spiced Lentil Pie

½ teaspoon coriander seeds
½ teaspoon whole cumin
½ teaspoon allspice berries
1 tablespoon sunflower oil
1 medium onion, peeled and chopped
1 clove garlic, peeled and crushed
8 oz (*225 g*) red lentils
1½ pints (*750 ml*) water
1 stick celery, diced
2 carrots, scrubbed and diced
bouquet garni

2 tablespoons tomato purée preserve
  (see page 147) (or bought tomato
  purée)
4 oz (*100 g*) lightly cooked sweetcorn
1 teaspoon fresh lovage, chopped
black pepper
1 lb (*450 g*) mashed potato

Herbs: lovage, bouquet garni

The secret of this recipe is to use whole spices, crushed and fried, for maximum flavour as often done in Indian cookery.

Method Crush the coriander, cumin and allspice in a mortar. Heat the oil in a large saucepan and fry the onion, garlic and crushed spices for 4–5 minutes, stirring constantly.

Add the lentils, water, celery, carrots and bouquet garni, bring to the boil and simmer for 35–40 minutes until the lentils are mushy and most of the moisture is absorbed.

Stir in the tomato purée, sweetcorn, lovage and a twist or two of freshly ground black pepper.

Turn into an ovenproof dish and cover with the mashed potato. Fork a pattern on top and bake at 425°F, 220°C, Gas 6, for about 20 minutes until the potato is nicely browned. (Serves 4)

Split Pea Slice

6 oz (*150 g*) green split peas
1 onion, peeled and chopped
1 grated carrot
2 oz (*50 g*) mushrooms, diced
2 oz (*50 g*) wholemeal breadcrumbs
1 tablespoon fresh mint, chopped
sprig of fresh tarragon (1 teaspoon if
  dried)
1 egg
1 teaspoon French mustard
freshly ground black pepper

Herbs: bouquet garni, mint, tarragon

Method   Soak the peas for 4–6 hours in cold water. Drain and put them in a pan with fresh water and the bouquet garni. Bring to the boil, then simmer, uncovered, for 40 minutes, topping up the water if necessary. Drain, and remove the bouquet garni. Add the remaining ingredients and mix thoroughly. Press into a 1 lb (*450 g*) loaf tin, lined with greased greaseproof paper, bake for 40–45 minutes, at 375°F, 190°C, Gas Mark 5, until firm and slightly browned on top.

Turn out and serve hot with vegetables and tomato and basil sauce (See page 146) or cold with a side salad. (Serves 4)

Lentil Loaf

Herbs: bouquet garni, marjoram, summer or winter savory

Follow the recipe for Split Pea Slice, substituting 6 oz (*150 g*) red lentils for the split peas – they will only need 15–20 minutes cooking time and no pre-soaking. They also absorb all the water so there is no need to drain. Use 3 teaspoons each of fresh chopped marjoram and savory (or 1 teaspoon each of dried) in place of the mint, and add 2 oz (*50 g*) grated low-fat Cheddar-type cheese to the other ingredients. (Serves 4)

Mexican Chilli Bean Stew

6 oz (*150 g*) red kidney beans
1 tablespoon olive oil
1 medium onion, peeled and
    chopped
2 cloves garlic, peeled and crushed
1 small aubergine, diced
1 lb (*450 g*) can chopped tomatoes
½–1 teaspoon chilli powder
small handful fresh coriander leaves
1 ripe avocado
1 tablespoon lemon juice

Herb: coriander

Coriander has a good spicy flavour which is robust enough not to be overpowered by the chilli.

This is a quick and easy dish to prepare and if you use canned kidney beans (drained and rinsed) it can be made in a matter of minutes.

Method   Soak the beans overnight. Drain and put them in a pan with fresh water to cover. Bring to the boil and boil rapidly for 10 minutes, then reduce the heat and simmer for a further 35–40 minutes.

Heat the oil in another pan and fry the onion, garlic and aubergine for 4–5 minutes. Add the drained beans, tomatoes, coriander and chilli powder and cook over a low heat for a further 5 minutes.

Peel and stone the avocado, cut up the flesh, squeeze lemon juice over it and add to the pan. Bring the stew back to simmering point and serve sprinkled with more freshly chopped coriander. Plain boiled rice and the yoghurt and cucumber mint relish (see page 148) would go well with this. (Serves 4)

Wholegrains, Nuts and Seeds

Grain or cereal crops include wheat, oats and rice.

If refined and over-processed grains lose essential nutrients as well as taste and texture. In their unrefined state (when known as whole grains), they retain the germ, which contains oils, proteins and minerals, and bran, which is a source of fibre. Nuts and seeds (botanically the same) are not only nutritious, providing protein, carbohydrate, fibre, fat, vitamins and minerals, but flavoursome as well. In combination with plenty of fresh herbs they can be used to give endless variety to dishes based on wholegrains.

Although nuts have a high fat content it is mostly unsaturated fat. (See page 13). Hazelnuts are comparatively low in fat, as are chestnuts, which, unlike most nuts, have a high starch content. These make good choices for dishes with nuts as a main ingredient.

The Recipes

		The herbs to include
1	*Orange Tabbouleh*	– parsley, mint, nasturtium
2	*Nutty Rice*	– borage, marjoram, chervil
3	*Spiced Vegetable Risotto*	– bay leaf, coriander
4	*Savoy Cabbage with Wild Rice Stuffing*	– basil, pot marigold
5	*Chestnut Loaf*	– rosemary
6	*Hazelnut Patties*	– sage, parsley

Orange Tabbouleh

4 oz (*100 g*) chick peas
8 oz (*250 g*) bulgar wheat
2 tablespoons olive or sunflower oil
1 tablespoon lemon juice
2 teaspoons orange flower water
4 spring onions, finely chopped
1 oz (*25 g*) flat-leaved parsley, finely
    chopped
8 sprigs mint, finely chopped
2 sweet oranges, peel, pith, seeds
    removed, finely sliced
1 small green pepper, half sliced, half
    cut into rings
nasturtium flowers

Herbs: flat-leaved parsley, mint, nasturtium flowers

This is a delightfully different, orange-scented version of the classic Middle Eastern dish.

The addition of chick peas makes it satisfying and nutritious. Bulgar wheat, also known as burghul, is a form of steamed, cracked wheat, which needs no further cooking.

Method   Soak the chick peas in water overnight. Drain and rinse them, then simmer in a pan of fresh water, for about one hour, or until tender, making sure that the first ten minutes of cooking time is at a full rolling boil.

Put the bulgar wheat in a bowl, cover with boiling water and leave for 20 minutes until all water is absorbed. Fluff up with a fork, then mix in the drained chick peas and all other ingredients, saving a few orange slices and the green pepper rings to go on top. Garnish with nasturtium flowers and eat cold as a salad. (Serves 4–6)

Nutty Rice

8 oz (325 g) brown rice
1¼ pints, (¾ litre) water
small handful fresh borage leaves
sprig of marjoram
1 tablespoon sunflower oil
2 oz (50 g) each of sesame seeds and
   sunflower seeds
1 stick of celery, cut into dice
1 green pepper, de-seeded and sliced
4 oz (100 g) mushrooms, sliced
2 oz (50 g) walnut pieces
2 oz (50 g) hazelnuts, roughly
   chopped
2 hard-boiled eggs, cut in quarters
1 dessertspoon chervil, finely
   chopped
a few borage flowers to garnish

Herbs: borage – leaves and flowers; marjoram; chervil

Brown rice has a nutty taste of its own which is brought out by the addition of nuts and seeds. Fresh borage leaves, cooked with the rice, make seasoning unnecessary and marjoram adds a warm, spicy flavour.

Method Put the rice, water, borage leaves and marjoram into a large pan. Bring to the boil, cover the pan tightly, reduce the heat, and simmer until the rice is tender but not mushy, about 20 minutes. Drain in a colander.

Heat the oil in a pan, add the sesame seeds, sunflower seeds, celery, green pepper and mushrooms and stir-fry for 2–3 minutes.

Turn the stir-fry mixture into the rice, with the walnuts and hazelnuts, and mix well together.

Turn into a serving dish and top with the quartered eggs. Sprinkle with the chervil and garnish with borage flowers. (Serves 4)

Spiced Vegetable Risotto

2 tablespoons sunflower oil
1 medium onion, peeled and
  chopped
2 cloves garlic, peeled and crushed
1 teaspoon coriander seeds
1 teasp cumin seeds
5–6 cardamom pods
1 teaspoon turmeric powder
8 oz (*225 g*) brown rice
1 pint (*600 ml*) water, or vegetable
  stock
1 tablespoon fresh coriander,
  chopped
pinch of salt, black pepper
Vegetables
2 carrots, diced
4 oz (*100 g*) sweetcorn
4 oz (*100 g*) broccoli florets
2 oz (*50 g*) shelled peas
2 tomatoes, chopped
1 sweet pepper

Herbs: bay leaf, coriander

If fresh coriander is difficult to come by – in winter perhaps – use fresh parsley instead, as the appearance and taste of this dish is greatly enhanced by the fresh green herb content. You can ring the changes by using different vegetables such as mange-tout peas, French or runner beans, baby sweetcorn, turnips, parsnips and cauliflower. Sliced water chestnuts (available in cans), add an interesting, crunchy texture.

Method   Heat the oil in a large, heavy-based saucepan and fry the onion and garlic gently for 2 minutes. Crush the coriander, cumin and cardamom coarsely, using a pestle and mortar, add to the pan and cook for a further 2 minutes, stirring all the time. Put in the rice, turning it for a few moments, until glistening, before adding the turmeric, seasoning, water and bay leaf. Bring to the boil and simmer for 10 minutes, then put in the prepared vegetables and finely chopped fresh coriander – reserving a little for garnish. Simmer for a further 10–15 minutes until the rice is cooked and all the liquid absorbed. Snip the remaining coriander over the risotto before serving. (Serves 4)

Savoy Cabbage with Wild Rice Stuffing

1 Savoy cabbage (2–2½ lbs [1 kilo] in weight)
4 oz (75 g) wild rice
1 pint (600 ml) water
4 oz (100 g) mushrooms
2 tablespoons olive oil
2 oz (50 g) mange-tout peas, cut in pieces
2 oz (50 g) sultanas
3 oz (75 g) mixed nuts (walnuts, cashews, hazelnuts, etc.)
1½ oz (40 g) mixed seeds (sunflower, sesame, pumpkin)
1 teaspoon juniper berries, crushed
grated nutmeg
½ teaspoon ground mace
salt and freshly ground black pepper
2–3 teaspoons fresh basil, finely chopped
petals from 3 pot marigold flowers, or 2 tablespoons dried petals
whole purple basil leaves for garnish

Herbs: green and purple basil, pot marigold petals

This dish takes a little time and trouble to prepare, but it makes a satisfyingly different centrepiece for a family occasion meal. I prefer to use Savoy cabbage because the texture and colour of the leaves are more appetising, when cooked, than most other varieties.

Although it is also a grass, wild rice is not really rice at all, but a completely different plant, *Zizania aquatica*, native to North America. It has a subtle and distinctive flavour, which is complemented but not overpowered by the basil. A few leaves of purple, as well as green basil, add colour contrast.

Method   Rinse the wild rice well and cook in the water for 50–60 minutes (20 minutes in a pressure cooker) until soft and the kernels have burst open.

Wash the cabbage carefully, discarding only the very outermost leaves. Blanch in a large pan of boiling water for 5 minutes. This is to make the leaves flexible. Remove from the water and drain. Fold back the outer leaves, exposing the heart. Cut this centre part out (it will still be hard). Chop half the cabbage heart, keeping the other half for use later.

Slice the mushrooms and sauté them lightly in the oil with the nuts and seeds. Mix mushrooms, nuts and seeds into the chopped cabbage leaves with the cooked wild rice and the rest of the ingredients, reserving some marigold petals for garnish.

Pile the stuffing mixture into the blanched cabbage shell, reform into a cabbage shape and tie in a net or muslin cloth (like a pudding bag). Cook in boiling water for a further 30 minutes. Turn the cabbage out carefully, remove the muslin, sprinkle with pot marigold petals and garnish with purple basil leaves. (Serves 4–6)

Chestnut Loaf

1 tablespoon olive oil
1 large onion, peeled and chopped
2 cloves garlic, peeled and crushed
1 stick celery, finely chopped
1 tablespoon wholemeal flour
8 oz (*230 g*) can chopped tomatoes in own juice
15 oz (*440 g*) can whole chestnuts, roughly chopped

2 oz (*50 g*) mixed chopped nuts and
   sunflower seeds
2 oz (*50 g*) wholemeal breadcrumbs
a sprig of rosemary, or 1 teaspoon
   dried rosemary
2 teaspoons soy sauce, or shoyu
salt and pepper to taste

Herb: rosemary

This makes a delicious winter treat, when both chestnuts and fresh rosemary are readily available. Whole canned chestnuts are more convenient to use than fresh ones, which must first be cooked and peeled. (Frozen or dried chestnuts are also suitable). For a smoother texture, mash or liquidise the chestnuts instead of chopping them up. If you buy ready-made chestnut purée make sure it is not sweetened.

Method   Heat the oil and gently cook the onion, garlic and celery in it for 3–4 minutes. Stir in the flour, then the chopped tomatoes, bring to the boil and stir until thickened. Now add the chestnuts, 1½ oz of the mixed nuts, breadcrumbs, 1 sprig of rosemary, soy sauce and seasoning and blend thoroughly. Spoon the mixture into a greased loaf tin and bake at 375°F, 190°C, Gas Mark 5, for 1–1¼ hours until firm. Put crumpled foil on top for the last 20 minutes to prevent overbrowning. Leave to stand in the tin for 10 minutes before turning out.

Serve hot garnished with rosemary and a few extra chopped mixed nuts, accompanied by vegetables and a homemade tomato sauce, or cold with salad. (Serves 4)

Hazelnut Patties

4 oz (*100 g*) hazelnuts
2 oz (*50 g*) wholemeal breadcrumbs
2 oz (*50 g*) rolled oats
1 onion, peeled and grated
1 tablespoon sesame oil
1 egg
1 teaspoon each fresh marjoram or
    oregano and sage, finely chopped
    (½ teaspoon each if dried)
½ teaspoon ground mace
1 teaspoon paprika
rolled oats (for coating)
oil for frying

Herbs: marjoram, sage

Any combination of mixed nuts can be used instead of hazelnuts alone. They need to be finely chopped or the patties do not hold together easily in the frying pan.

Method   Chop the hazelnuts, or grind briefly in a food processor. Mix all the ingredients together, then (with well-floured hands) form into little cakes, coat each one with rolled oats and shallow fry for 5–6 minutes on each side. Delicious hot or cold. (Makes 8–10 patties)

Pizzas, Pastas and Pancakes

The recipes in this section depend for their success on the interest of the sauce or filling. This is where herbs are invaluable. Traditional pasta herbs – warm spicy basil and oregano – are ideal. Lovage and fennel are more unexpected and their distinctive flavours make a pleasant change. The pasta receipes give quantities for the dried product, which swells in the cooking. If you use the delicious, fresh pastas, now available, you will need about double the quantities given.

The Recipes

			the herbs to include
1	*Quick-Bake Pizza*	–	marjoram/oregano, basil
2	*Wholewheat Spaghetti with Ratatouille Sauce*	–	basil
3	*Spinach Lasagne*	–	parsley, lovage
4	*Tagliatelle with Fennel & Almonds*	–	fennel
5	*Savoury Stuffed Pancakes Broccoli & Beansprout Spinach, Sorrel & Sesame Seed*	–	borage, savory sorrel
6	*Mushroom & Pepper Pasta Salad*		tarragon, dill, nasturtium seeds

Quick-Bake Pizza

Base
4 oz (*100 g*) wholemeal flour
2 teaspoons baking powder
1 tablespoon olive or sunflower oil
1 teaspoon dried oregano
pinch of garlic salt
water to mix
Topping
8 oz (*225 g*) can Italian plum tomatoes
1 tablespoon tomato purée
2 oz (*50 g*) Mozzarella cheese, grated
4–5 leaves fresh basil, finely chopped
8–10 black olives
7 oz (*185 g*) can red pimientos (sweet red peppers)

Herbs: dried oregano or marjoram, fresh basil

A scone-type dough makes an excellent base for pizza and is quicker and easier to prepare than the more traditional one based on yeast. For a crunchy base, a flat, round or oval wholemeal loaf, cut in half and with some of the crumb removed, makes a tasty alternative.

You can, of course, use low-fat Edam or Cheddar in place of Mozarella cheese, but the result will not be as good.

Method (Base)   Sieve the flour into a bowl with the baking powder, oregano and garlic salt. Add the oil and enough water to make a soft dough. Roll out on a floured board into a circular shape, about ½ inch (*1 cm*) thick. Put this on a greased baking tray.

To make the topping   Put the tomatoes and tomato purée in a small pan with the basil and cook gently until pulped and well reduced. Spread this mixture on the base, cover with the grated cheese and arrange the olives and sliced pimiento on top. Drizzle a little more olive oil over the pizza and bake at 425°F, 220°C, Gas Mark 7, for 15–20 minutes.

Whole-wheat Spaghetti with Ratatouille Sauce*

2 oz (*50 g*) wholewheat spaghetti per serving

For the Sauce (to serve 4–6)

2 medium aubergines
2 medium onions, peeled and sliced
2 cloves garlic, peeled and crushed
4 small courgettes, cut into chunks
1 green, or red, pepper, de-seeded, cored and sliced
4 tomatoes, cut in eighths
2 tablespoons tomato purée preserve (see page 147) (or bought tomato puree)
mixed into ½ pint (*300 ml*) water
black pepper
8 fresh basil leaves, finely chopped
4 tablespoons sunflower or basil-flavoured oil

Herb: basil

When fresh basil is not available, you can get a very good flavour by using basil oil (see page 72) and frozen basil leaves.

Leave out the tomato purée and water and this sauce makes an excellent ratatouille to serve on its own as a starter, or as an accompaniment to a main course.

Method   First make the sauce Remove the stalks and cut the aubergines into roughly ½ inch (*2 cm*) cubes. Put them in a colander, sprinkle with salt, put a weighted plate on top and leave for at least 30 minutes. Rinse the aubergines well, to remove all traces of salt, and pat dry with plenty of paper towel – this process removes any bitterness.

Heat the oil in a saucepan, add the onions and garlic and cook for 5 minutes over a low heat. Add the rest of the prepared vegetables and cook for a further 5 minutes. Next add the tomato purée and water and some freshly ground black pepper to taste.

Cover the pan and cook for a further 25–30 minutes, adding the basil in the last 5 minutes of cooking time.

The spaghetti Cook the spaghetti in plenty of boiling water in a large saucepan for 15–20 minutes, until just tender. Drain, and serve topped with the sauce and a little extra snipped fresh basil.

Spinach Lasagne

8 oz (225 g) wholewheat lasagne
1 lb (450 g) spinach
4 oz (100 g) fromage frais
grated nutmeg
Sauce
1 oz (25 g) polyunsaturated margarine
1 oz (25 g) wholewheat flour
1 pint skimmed milk
4 oz (100 g) low-fat Edam cheese
½ oz (15 g) parsley, finely chopped
5–6 lovage leaves, finely chopped
salt and pepper

Herbs: parsley, lovage

Method

Cook the lasagne for about 10 minutes, or until just tender, in plenty of boiling water. Drain, and put it into a bowl of cold water so that the strips don't stick together.

Cook the spinach for 8 minutes – steam, or boil it in a pan with a scant tablespoon of water. Then drain well and mash the spinach together with the fromage frais and grated nutmeg to taste.

Make the sauce by melting the margarine, stirring in the flour and cooking for 1 minute, then removing from the heat and adding the milk, cheese, parsley, lovage and seasoning. Finally, bring the sauce back to the boil and stir until thickened.

115

To Assemble: Build up layers of lasagne, spinach and sauce in a square, shallow casserole dish, finishing with a layer of lasagne topped by sauce. Sprinkle with paprika and bake in a moderate oven, 350°F, 180°C, Gas mark 4, for 35–40 minutes until hot through and bubbly on top. (Serves 4–6)

Tagliatelle with Fennel and Almonds

8 oz (225 g) wholewheat tagliatelle, or tagliatelle verdi
Sauce
1 tablespoon olive or sunflower oil
1 onion, peeled and chopped
2 cloves garlic, peeled and crushed
1 stick celery, finely chopped
1 head Florence fennel, thinly sliced
½ a sweet red pepper, ½ a yellow pepper, cut in strips
2 oz (50 g) flaked almonds, lightly toasted
1 lb (250 g) fromage frais
2–3 fennel leaves
salt and pepper

Herb: fennel

Fresh tagliatelle, which cooks in 3–4 minutes, is nicest for this recipe. Tagliatelle verdi, which includes dried spinach, has an appetising green colour which goes well with the sauce.

Method (Sauce)   Heat the oil in a pan, put in the onion and cook for 2–3 minutes. Then add the garlic, celery, sweet pepper and fennel, cover and cook gently for a further 8 minutes, stirring occasionally. Mix in the fromage frais, a pinch of salt and freshly ground black pepper. Heat to just below boiling point. Add the almonds, reserving a few for garnish.

Meanwhile cook the tagliatelle until just tender, according to the instructions on the pack. Drain, and serve with the sauce, garnished with snipped fresh fennel leaves and almonds. (Serves 4)

Savoury Stuffed Pancakes

Pancakes
4 oz (*100 g*) wholewheat flour
1 egg
½ pint (*300 ml*) skimmed milk
oil, or margarine, for frying

Method Put the flour in a bowl, break in the egg and start to mix in in, then add the milk gradually, blending to a smooth batter. Heat the oil in a frying pan, pour in 2 tablespoons of batter, tipping the pan so the mixture spreads evenly. Cook for 2–3 minutes on each side. Continue until you have used up all the batter (this quantity makes about 8). Keep the pancakes warm in a low oven while you make the filling.

To assemble Spoon some of the prepared filling into the centre of each pancake, folding the ends over to enclose it.

Broccoli and Beansprout Filling

1 tablespoon sesame oil
1 tablespoon sunflower oil
8 oz (*225 g*) beansprouts
8 oz (*225 g*) broccoli florets
8 oz (*225 g*) can of pineapple pieces in own juice
½ inch (*1 cm*) cube of fresh root ginger, finely chopped
1 clove garlic, peeled and crushed
3–4 young borage leaves, shredded
2–3 teaspoons fresh summer savory leaves

117

Herbs: borage, summer savory

Method   Heat the oils in a frying pan. Strain the juice from the pineapple pieces and add them to the pan with all the other ingredients. Stir-fry for 2–3 minutes. (Fills 8 pancakes)

Spinach, Sorrel and Sesame Seed Filling

12 oz (325 g) spinach
1 oz (25 g) polyunsaturated
   margarine
8 oz (225 g) French sorrel
freshly ground black pepper
¼ nutmeg, freshly grated
5 oz (125 g) plain low-fat yoghurt
12 oz (325 g) curd cheese, or fromage
   frais
1 oz (25 g) sesame seeds, lightly
   toasted under a grill

Herb: sorrel

Method   Steam the spinach for 6–8 minutes, then cut through it in all directions with a knife. Heat the margarine in a saucepan. Put in the sorrel and cook for 3–4 minutes, until it has collapsed and darkened in colour, stirring to prevent it sticking. Blend the yoghurt and curd cheese together and stir into the sorrel, along with the sesame seeds and cooked spinach. Season with nutmeg and pepper. (Fills 8 pancakes)

Mushroom Pasta Salad

6 oz (*150 g*) wholewheat pasta shells
6 oz (*150 g*) large, flat mushrooms, lightly poached in white wine or vegetable stock
1 sweet red pepper, sliced and blanched in boiling water for 1 minute
5 oz (*125 g*) plain yoghurt
1 tablespoon low-fat mayonnaise
12 stoned black olives
3 oz (*75 g*) raisins, soaked in boiling water for 10 minutes
2–3 teaspoons pickled nasturtium seeds
4 to 5 basil leaves, finely chopped
small bunch of dill leaves, finely chopped
1 teaspoon dill seeds, crushed
seasoning to taste

Herbs: basil, dill, pickled nasturtium seeds

Pickled nasturtium seeds provide an interesting piquancy to this salad and are easy to prepare. Simply put freshly gathered nasturtium seeds into a screw-top glass jar, with a tablespoon of mixed pickling spice tied in muslin, and cover with cider or wine vinegar. Leave for a few weeks before using.

Method   Cook the pasta shells according to the instructions on the pack. Drain and rinse in cold water.

Combine the yoghurt and mayonnaise. Cut up the poached mushrooms, drain the red pepper and raisins and mix into the pasta shells with all the other ingredients. (Serves 4)

Cheese and Eggs

Low-fat dairy products, and eggs eaten in moderation, add variety to the diet and are a good source of essential nutrients. They provide protein, minerals, including calcium, and some vitamins. Skimming the fat off milk removes only a little vitamin D and A, which can be obtained in other ways. (Vitamin D from sunlight, vitamin A from carrots and green vegetables). Eggs contain iron and some of the B vitamins as well as calcium and vitamin A. All the cheeses mentioned are available in vegetarian versions, free from animal rennet. Look out for the Vegetarian Society V symbol on packaging. A list of suppliers of vegetarian cheeses can be obtained by sending a stamped addressed envelope to: The Vegetarian Society, Parkdale, Dunham Road, Altrincham, Cheshire WA14 4QG.

The Recipes

		the herbs to include
1	Chef's Salad with Cheese and Tofu	– bay leaf, hyssop, borage, mint
2	Pistachio Asparagus Terrine	– summer savory
3	Courgette Quiche	– dill
4	Spanish Omelette	– parsley, chervil, tarragon, chives
5	Tarragon and Tomato Baked Eggs	– tarragon

Chef's Salad with Cheese and Tofu

4 oz (*100 g*) firm tofu, cut into small cubes
4 oz (*100 g*) low-fat Cheddar or Edam cheese, cut into cubes
2 oz (*50 g*) walnut pieces
Mixed salad leaves, shredded – lettuce, endive, salad rocket, young dandelion leaves, radiccio
1 head Florence fennel, thinly sliced
8 oz (*225 g*) mange-tout peas or whole green beans, blanched
a few hyssop leaves and flowers
a few borage leaves, chopped, and flowers
6–8 mint leaves, chopped
For the marinade
3 tablespoons walnut oil
3 tablespoons lemon juice
2 tablespoons dry sherry
1 tablespoon light soy sauce, or shoyu
2 cloves crushed garlic
6 crushed peppercorns
bayleaf

Herbs: bayleaf, hyssop, borage, mint

Tofu is a low-fat, high-protein product of the soya bean, rich in calcium. It is available in firm and soft (often labelled as silken) textures. A firm textured tofu is best for this recipe. For a special occasion the addition of hard-boiled quail's eggs provides a touch of luxury.

Method   Mix all the marinade ingredients together in a bowl, add the tofu and cheese and leave for 3-4 hours.

Mix the salad leaves, fennel, peas or beans and herbs in a large bowl. Add the tofu and cheese, removed from the marinade,

121

add the walnuts. Just before serving toss the salad in half the strained marinade, and decorate with hyssop and borage flowers. (Serves 4)

Pistachio Asparagus Terrine

6 asparagus spears (or 4 oz broccoli florets)
8 oz (*100 g*) quark or fromage frais (1 tablespoon for topping)
1 tablespoon flour
3 fl oz (*100 ml*) skimmed milk
1 egg
grated rind and juice of ½ a lemon
3 teaspoons fresh summer savory
2 oz (*50 g*) pistachios (1 oz peeled and halved, 1 oz finely chopped)

Herb: summer savory

This is a light and elegant dish, ideal for serving with summer salads.

Method   Grease and line a 1 lb (*450 g*) loaf tin. Blanch the asparagus (or broccoli), in boiling water for 2 minutes. Blend the fromage frais, flour, milk, lemon, egg and herbs together, until smooth – a food processor makes the job easier. Pour one third of this mixture into the prepared loaf tin. Reserving the chopped pistachios for the topping, put in half the remainder of the pistachios and 3 asparagus spears, cover with more fromage frais mixture, then more pistachios and asparagus and a final layer of mixture. Bake in a pre-heated oven, at 350°F, 180°C, Gas Mark 4, for 1–1¼ hours until set and lightly golden on top. Leave in the tin for ten minutes before turning out. When cold, spread a little fromage frais on top and decorate with chopped pistachio nuts. (Serves 4)

Courgette Quiche

Pastry Case
4 oz (100 g) wholemeal flour
2 oz (50 g) plain white flour
3 oz (75 g) margarine
water to mix

A little white flour in the pastry crust and the beaten egg white in the filling makes this quiche as light and puffy as a soufflé. You can use plain cottage cheese, but the flavoured one specified gives a tastier result.

Method Sieve the flours into a bowl, adding the bran that will be left in the sieve. Rub in the margarine and add enough water to make an elastic dough. Roll it out on a floured board to fit an 8 in (20 cm) flan ring, or loose-bottomed sandwich tin. Press the pastry firmly into place and patch if necessary (it will be quite soft).

Prick the pastry base all over with a fork and bake at 350°F, 180°C, Gas Mark 4 for 10 minutes.

Filling
8 oz (225 g) courgettes, sliced
a few sprays of dill and ½ teaspoon
    dill seeds, crushed
3 oz (75 g) 'cottage cheese with
    onions and cheddar'
2 eggs
¼ pint (150 ml) skimmed milk
1 teaspoon paprika, salt and pepper
    to taste

Herb: dill

Method Arrange the courgettes in the partially cooked flan case. Sprinkle with dill seeds and finely snipped dill leaf. Separate one of the eggs and whisk the white until stiff but not dry. Beat the yolk with the other egg, add the milk, cottage cheese and seasonings, then gently mix in the egg white. Pour the egg and milk mixture over the courgettes, return to the oven and bake, at the same temperature as before, for about 40 minutes until set and golden brown. (Serves 4)

123

Spanish Omelette

6 eggs
4 medium potatoes, peeled and diced
2 medium onions, peeled and sliced
3 tablespoons olive oil
salt and freshly ground black pepper
2 teaspoons each parsley and chervil,
    finely chopped
1 teaspoon each tarragon and chives,
    finely chopped

Herbs: parsley, chervil, tarragon and chives

The classic Spanish omelette is a simple dish which does not contain peppers, peas or any other such distractions. This recipe came from Fernando of the Sombrero Bar, Los Boliches. I have given it a French accent by the addition of *fines herbes*.

Method   Heat 2 tablespoons of the oil in a frying pan. Put in the onions and potatoes, cover with a well-fitting lid and cook gently until the vegetables are tender but not brown, stirring occasionally.

Whisk the eggs in a large bowl and add the vegetable mixture, seasoning and herbs. Wipe out the pan, heat the remaining tablespoon of oil, add the omelette mixture and cook briskly until lightly browned underneath.

Put a plate over the pan and invert the omelette on to it. Return the pan to the heat (you may need just a touch more oil), slide the omelette, uncooked side down, back into the pan and cook until golden and set. (Serves 4)

Sweet Treats

A diet which allows for no sweet things at all becomes a very dull affair indeed, so this section is devoted to special occasion 'sweet treats'.

Once again herbs come to the rescue. Some of them are a great help when it comes to cutting down on sugar, which is, in any case, added with a very light hand in the following recipes. And remember, just as it is possible to get used to the taste of less salt in the diet, so can a taste be acquired for less sugar.

The Recipes

		the herbs to include
1	*Rhubarb & Angelica Crumble*	– angelica
2	*Summer Charlotte*	– sweet cicely
3	*Gooseberry & Elderflower* Soufflé	– sweet cicely
4	*Blackcurrant & Peppermint Sorbet*	– peppermint, sweet cicely
5	*Rose Petal Cheesecake*	– rose petals
6	*Rose Petal Yoghurt Syllabub*	– rose petals
7	*Citrus Fruit Salad*	– lemon balm, pot marigold petals to garnish
8	*Apricot & Lemon Balm Purée*	– lemon balm, borage flowers
9	*Dried Fruit Compôte*	– rosemary nasturtium flowers and rosemary flowers to garnish

Rhubarb & Angelica Crumble

1½ lbs (*600 g*) rhubarb
2 x 6in (*15 cm*) stems young angelica
2 oz (*50 g*) demarara sugar
juice of 1 orange

For the Crumble Topping

1 oz (*25 g*) polyunsaturated margarine
2 oz (*50 g*) stoned dates
3 oz (*75 g*) fruit and nut muesli (with no added sugar)
2 oz (*50 g*) rolled oats
grated rind of 1 orange

Herb: angelica

If you have always disliked the tart aftertaste of rhubarb, try cooking it with angelica. It works by reducing the acidity of the fruit and means that you will need to add far less sugar than is usually necessary.

Method Cut the rhubarb and angelica into even 2 in (*5 cm*) chunks and put into an ovenproof dish. Sprinkle with the sugar and stir in the orange juice.

For the Topping: Melt the margarine in a saucepan. Cut up the dates, add them to the pan and cook, stirring with a wooden spoon, for 2–3 mins. Add the muesli, rolled oats and orange rind. Spread this topping mixture over the rhubarb and angelica.

Bake in a moderate oven (375°F, 190°C, Gas Mark 5) until the rhubarb is cooked and the crumble topping brown – about 40–45 minutes. To prevent the topping over-browning, cover with foil after 20 minutes cooking time. (Serves 4)

Summer Charlotte

1 lb (*450 g*) mixed soft fruits – choose from blackcurrants, redcurrants, raspberries, strawberries, loganberries, blackberries, stoned cherries
2–3 sweet cicely leaves
2 oz (*50 g*) brown sugar
4 oz (*100 g*) fresh brown breadcrumbs
2 oz (*50 g*) mixed finely chopped nuts
1 tablespoon sunflower oil
yoghurt and honey to serve

Herb: sweet cicely

Sweet cicely really does have a sweet taste and is an invaluable herb for the repertoire of the health-conscious cook. Its pretty fern-like leaves always make an attractive garnish for a sweet dish. Make sure you have the real thing, though, and don't pick it from the wild as it bears a passing resemblance to fool's parsley and other such plants – which can be poisonous.

Method   Shred the sweet cicely leaves, reserving a whole piece for garnish, and mix them into the soft fruits with 1 oz of the sugar. Mix together the breadcrumbs, chopped nuts, sunflower oil and remaining sugar.

Put alternate layers of soft fruits and breadcrumb mixture into a pie-dish, starting with fruit and finishing with a layer of breadcrumbs.

Bake at 375°F, 190°C, Gas Mark 5, for 35–40 minutes.

Remove from the oven, decorate with the reserved sweet cicely leaf and serve with yoghurt sweetened with a little honey. (Serves 4)

Goose- berry and Elderflower Soufflé

3 oz (75 g) sugar
¼ pint (150 ml) water
1 lb (450 g gooseberries
2 heads of elderflower, or tablespoon dried elderflowers
3–4 sprays of sweet cicely
1 sachet agar-jelly
¼ pint (150 ml) orange juice
2 large eggs, separated
1 oz (25 g) pistachio nuts

Herb: sweet cicely

This makes a lovely creamy soufflé – but without the cream! The muscatel flavour of the elderflowers complements the taste of the gooseberries. Dried elderflowers make a very satisfactory substitute when the fresh ones are not in season.

Method   In an enamelled pan dissolve 2 oz (50 g of the sugar in ¼ pint (150 ml) water over a low heat. Strip the elderflowers from their stalks and put them into the pan with the gooseberries and sweet cicely leaves (reserving some for decoration).

Simmer gently until tender – 10–15 minutes. Liquidise the fruit, in a food processor or blender, then push it through a fine nylon sieve, to remove pips and stalks, into a large bowl.

Put the agar-jelly in a pan with the orange juice and bring to boiling point, while stirring. Remove from the heat. Put the egg yolks and remaining sugar into a small bowl and whisk over a pan of hot water until thick and creamy. Stir the yolk mixture into the gooseberry purée, along with the agar liquid.

Put in the refrigerator until on the point of setting.

Meanwhile prepare a 1-pint (600 ml) capacity soufflé dish by tying around it a band of doubled, very lightly-oiled greaseproof paper, so that about 2½ inches (60 cm) stands above the rim of the dish.

Beat the egg-whites until stiff and fold them into the almost set purée. Pour the mixture into the prepared soufflé dish and leave to set, preferably overnight.

Remove the paper before serving and decorate the sides and top with chopped pistachio nuts and sweet cicely leaves. (Serves 4)

Black-currant and Pepper-mint Sorbet

2 oz (50 g) sugar
½ pint (300 ml) water
1 lb (450 g) blackcurrants
large bunch peppermint leaves
   (about 6 stems)
spray of sweet cicely leaves
1 tablespoon cassis liqueur (optional)

Herbs: peppermint, sweet cicely

Although each serving would contain only a modest amount of liqueur, the cassis *can* be left out if you want to keep the sugar content to a minimum. For the best flavour, be sure to use peppermint in this recipe rather than spearmint or applemint.

Method Dissolve the sugar in the water in an enamelled saucepan. Add the blackcurrants, sweet cicely leaves and half the bunch of peppermint leaves and simmer over a gentle heat until tender – about 10 mins. Remove the herbs and press the fruit through a sieve to make a purée. Finely chop the rest of the peppermint leaves and mix them into the purée with the cassis if using.

Pour into an ice-making tray, or plastic 'fridge box, and put in the freezer, until the sorbet is frozen at the edges. Remove from the freezer, scrape into a bowl and beat thoroughly with an electric mixer (or blend in a food processor) until frothy and mushy. Return to the freezing tray and freeze until solid.

Remove from the freezer 5 minutes before required to soften a little and serve in individual glasses decorated with a few whole blackcurrants and peppermint leaves. (Serves 4)

Rose-Petal Cheesecake

For the Base

6 oz (*150 g*) digestive biscuits
½ teaspoon cinnamon powder
2 oz (*50 g*) polyunsaturated
  margarine

For the Filling

12 oz (*325 g*) curd cheese
4 oz (*100 g*) fromage frais
3 oz (*75 g*) castor sugar
1 lemon, rind and juice
1 tablespoon distilled rose-water
petals of 2 fragrant pink or red roses

For the Topping

Petals from 2 fragrant red roses
¼ pint (*150 ml*) water
1 teaspoon arrowroot
1–2 level tablespoons sugar
1 teaspoon distilled rose-water

Herb: rose petals

This low-fat cheesecake is my very favourite summertime recipe and never fails to draw a compliment.

The little white bit at the base of each rose petal, visible when they are pulled apart, is slightly bitter and it is worth the trouble of snipping each one out with a pair of sharp scissors.

Method For the Base Crush the biscuits, not too finely. An easy way to do this is to put them in a plastic bag and squash with a rolling-pin. Melt the margarine in a pan and stir in the biscuits and cinnamon. Press the biscuit mixture into the base of a loose-bottomed 8 inch (*20 cm*) cake tin.

For the Filling Beat together the cheeses, castor sugar and grated lemon rind. Stir in the rose-water.

Cut the white 'heel' out of each rose-petal wich scissors, then snip the petals into the cheese mixture and mix them in. Pour the filling onto the base and chill overnight.

For the Topping Put the rose petals into a jug, reserving a few for decoration. Pour the boiling water over the petals, cover the jug and leave to infuse for 1 hour.

Strain out the petals. Mix the arrowroot to a thin paste with a little of the infused rosewater.

Stir the paste into the rest of the rose infusion and put into a pan with the sugar. Bring very slowly to the boil and stir until thickened. Mix in the distilled rosewater. Spread the topping over the cheese-cake and decorate with the remaining rose-petals. (Serves 4–6)

Rose-Petal Yoghurt Syllabub

10 oz (*275 g*) plain yoghurt
1 tablespoon honey
2 teaspoons lemon juice
1 tablespoon skimmed milk powder
2 egg-whites stiffly beaten
1 tablespoon distilled rosewater
petals from 2 fragrant pink or red
  roses
¼ freshly grated nutmeg
grated rind of ½ a lemon

Herb: rose petals

In Elizabethan days syllabub was a froth made by milking thick, creamy milk straight from the cow into a jug of wine! This light and low-fat modern equivalent makes use of yoghurt, thickened with skimmed milk powder, and is 'frothed' with egg-whites.

Method Put the yoghurt into a mixing bowl and beat in the honey, lemon juice, skimmed milk powder and rosewater. Fold in the stiffly beaten egg-whites and snipped rose-petals, from which the white 'heels' at the base have been removed.

Turn the syllabub into a serving bowl and decorate with a few more rose-petals and a sprinkling of grated nutmeg and lemon rind. (Serves 3–4)

Citrus Fruit Salad

2–3 oranges
3–4 satsumas
1 grapefruit
4 oz (*100 g*) dates, stoned and chopped
½ pint (*300 ml*) water
6–8 lemon balm leaves
petals from 1 pot marigold head
rosemary flowers

Herbs: lemon balm, (sweet cicely); to garnish: pot marigold petals; rosemary flowers

The fresh taste of lemon balm goes especially well with fruit salads, and pot marigold petals add a bright finishing touch. The sweetness in this recipe is provided by the dates. You could also use a little finely chopped sweet cicely.

Method　Peel the fruit, removing all the pith. Divide the satsumas into segments. Finely slice the oranges and grapefruit, taking care to remove all pips, then cut each slice into 4 pieces. Place in a glass serving dish.

Put the dates into a saucepan with ¼ pint (*150 ml*) of the water, snip in the lemon balm leaves, bring to the boil and simmer, stirring and pressing the dates with a wooden spoon for 4–5 minutes until they are pulped.

Add the rest of the water, bring briefly to the boil then strain the date mixture through a sieve. Pour it over the fruit and sprinkle with pot marigold petals, rosemary flowers and finely chopped sweet cicely, if using. (Serves 6)

Apricot and Lemon Balm Purée

8 oz (*225 g*) dried apricots
small bunch lemon balm leaves
(about 6 stems)
5 oz (*125 g*) plain yoghurt
2 tablespoons honey
1 oz (*50 g*) skimmed milk powder
1 oz (*50 g*) ground almonds
½ teaspoon dried ginger

Herb: lemon balm, borage flowers

Lemon balm, or melissa, gives this purée of dried apricots a lovely fresh taste and the bright-blue borage stars make an unusual garnish.

Method Soak the apricots overnight in cold water. Put them in a pan with half the bunch of lemon balm. Cook for 10–15 minutes until soft.

Drain well, remove lemon balm, then put the apricots into a blender or food processor with the remaining lemon balm leaves stripped from their stalks and all the other ingredients and process until well combined. (Alternatively, press the apricots through a sieve and mix well with the other ingredients).

Serve well chilled in individual glasses topped with fresh (or crystallized) borage flowers. (Serves 4)

Dried Fruit Compôte

8 oz (*225 g*) mixed dried fruit
(apricots, apples, pears, peaches,
prunes etc.)
2 oz sultanas
small sprig of rosemary
1 orange, grated rind and juice
1 tablespoon honey (optional)
3–5 nasturtium flowers
rosemary flowers

Herbs: rosemary; nasturtium flowers for decoration

A discreet hint of rosemary gives this dish zest. Nasturtium flowers *are* edible, but are really there for their decorative vlaue and bright sun colours.

Method   Soak the dried fruit overnight in cold water.

Next day put it into a pan with the sultanas, the sprig of rosemary, grated orange rind and honey if using. Simmer over a gentle heat until the fruit is tender – about 10 minutes. Turn into a serving dish, pour in the orange juice and garnish with rosemary flowers and nasturtiums. (Serves 4)

Herb Cheeses

Soft white cheeses, such as cottage and curd, have a remarkably low fat content – between 4–10% in fact. They can be rather bland however, and lend themselves to being mixed with herbs. Quark, a low-fat German white cheese, has a lovely light texture and is usually made with skimmed or semi-skimmed milk – but check the label as there are some higher-fat versions on the market.

Don't be tempted to go for cream cheeses, which are as high in fat as Cheddar and Stilton at 35–50% fat.

Edam and French cheeses such as Brie and Camembert have a medium fat content – 20–25% – and make a pleasant occasional change. The special low-fat Cheddar-type cheeses, now available, are also worth trying with a fat content of only 15–16%.

The Recipes

the herbs to include

1 *Soft White Cheese with with Mixed Fresh Herbs*
   1) *fines herbes* – (parsley, chives, tarragon, chervil)
   2) basil, French parsley
   3) lovage, mint, marjoram
   4) rosemary, thyme, marjoram
   5) savory, dill seeds

2 *Spiced Marigold Curd Cheese* pot marigold

3 *Potted Sage Cheese* sage

4 *Brie with Garlic and Chives* chives

5 *Savory Cheese Bites* summer or winter savory

6 Yoghurt Herb Cheese lemon thyme, marjoram

Soft White Cheese with Mixed Fresh Herbs

8 oz (225 g) carton low-fat soft white cheese

2 tablespoons fresh, or frozen, *fines herbes* – (see page 15 for proportions)

The classic *fines herbes* combination – parsley, chives, tarragon and chervil – is hard to beat for a standard soft white cheese with herbs. Curd, cottage, or low-fat quark are all suitable.

Method Turn the cheese into a bowl, thoroughly incorporate the finely-chopped herbs, then press into a small pâté dish, or replace in the original carton.

There is plenty of scope for inventiveness and to try out your own ideas but below are a few more tried and tested herb combinations. All the herbs should be fresh (or frozen) and finely chopped, except where dried are specified.

For 8 oz (225 g) soft white cheese:
1. 3 teaspoons basil
   3 teaspoons French, or flat-leaved parsley

2. 1 teaspoon lovage
   3 teaspoons mint
   3 teaspoons marjoram

    3 2 teaspoons rosemary
       3 teaspoons thyme OR 1 teaspoon of each dried
       3 teaspoons marjoram
    4 3 teaspoons dried savory
       1 teaspoon crushed dill seeds

For contrast in flavour and colour serve the following two cheeses
together.

Spiced Marigold Curd Cheese

4 oz (*100 g*) curd cheese
petals from half a head of pot
    marigold OR 2 teaspoons dried pot
    marigold petals
½ teaspoon cinnamon
sprinkling of freshly grated nutmeg
2–3 teaspoons fresh orange juice

Herb: pot marigold

Method   Reserving 5 for decoration, crush the pot marigold petals
in a mortar until the juice runs, then beat them into the cheese
with the remaining ingredients. (If using dried petals, simply beat
them in without first crushing).

Press into a ramekin dish and top with the reserved petals
arranged in a star shape.

Potted Sage Cheese

8 oz (225 g) grated Edam or low-fat
  Cheddar-type cheese
2 tablespoons finely chopped sage
1 tablespoon dry white wine or dry
  sherry

Herb: sage

Method   Put all the ingredients into a small heavy-based pan and stir over a very low heat until the cheese is melted and has taken on the colour of the sage. Put into a ramekin dish and leave to set. Or put into small sterilised jars, cover with air-tight lids, or seal with jam-pot covers and eat within three weeks.

Brie with Chives and Garlic

4 oz (100 g) Brie
1 tablespoon finely chopped chives
1 small clove garlic
2 tablespoons skimmed milk

Herb: chives

A deliciously creamy herb cheese with a really fresh chive flavour. The garlic can be left out if you find it a little over-powering.

Method   Cut the Brie into small cubes and put in a heavy-based pan with the chives and skimmed milk. Add the garlic, pushed through a garlic press, and stir the mixture over a very low heat until the cheese has melted. Heat, without boiling, for 2–3 minutes.

Pour into a ramekin dish, or small pâté dish, and leave at room temperature until solid.

Savory Cheese Bites

8 oz (*200 g*) curd cheese
1 tablespoon paprika
1 tablespoon summer savory, finely
  chopped

Herb: summer or winter savory

These are good served with an aperitif instead of salted peanuts or crisps.

Method Using a teaspoon, scoop out small portions of curd cheese and roll into walnut-sized balls.

Put the paprika and savory on two separate saucers. Roll each ball first in paprika then in the fresh herb.

Arrange on a dish lined with angelica leaves.

Yoghurt Herb Cheese

1 lb (*500 g*) plain yoghurt
2 teaspoons fresh lemon thyme
1 teaspoon fresh marjoram, finely
  chopped (OR 3 teaspoons in all of
  any of the combinations of herbs
  given on page 47)
1 teaspoon paprika

Herbs: lemon thyme, marjoram

This is very simple to do if you have a 'jelly-bag' and, if you make your own yoghurt, most economical.

Method Put the yoghurt in a jelly-bag, or square of muslin, suspended over a basin and leave for several hours, or overnight until all liquid is drained off. Mix in the finely chopped fresh herbs and sprinkle with paprika.

Dips

Served with a variety of crunchy, raw vegetables, bread sticks or home-made biscuits, dips make much more healthy nibbles than fatty, salt-laden crisps or roast peanuts.

Choose from dips based on soft cheese or cooked creamy beans and add fresh herbs for flavour and interest.

The Recipes

		the herbs to include
1	*Creamy Cheese Dip with* Fines Herbes	– *fines herbes* – (parsley, chives, tarragon, chervil)
2	*Apricot and Mint Dip*	– spearmint or applemint sweet cicely
3	*Two-Bean Dip*	– bouquet garni – (of bay leaf, parsley, thyme, summer or winter savory)
4	*Hummus*	– parsley

Creamy Cheese Dip with Fines Herbes

8 oz (225 g) low-fat quark
2 tablespoons low-fat mayonnaise
1 tablespoon plain yoghurt
1 tablespoon fresh or frozen *fines herbes* (see page 47)
1 teaspoon lemon juice
½ teaspoon coriander powder

Herbs: *fines herbes* (parsley, chives, tarragon, chervil)

You could, of course, try other combinations of herbs in this dip – see the suggestions for soft cheese with mixed fresh herbs. (page 47)

Method   Mix all the ingredients together until well combined. (Serves 4–6)

Apricot and Mint Dip

4 oz (100 g) dried apricots
spray of sweet cicely leaves
small bunch mint leaves
6 oz (150 g) curd cheese
2 oz (50 g) plain yoghurt
1 teaspoon paprika
extra sweet cicely for garnish

Herb: spearmint or applemint, sweet cicely

Method   Soak the apricots overnight in cold water. Next day, turn into a saucepan, add the herbs and cook gently for 10–12 minutes, until tender.

Remove the herbs, drain the apricots well and leave to cool, then place in a liquidizer or food processor with the remaining ingredients and blend to a purée. Serve garnished with a spray of sweet cicely. (Serves 4–6)

Two-Bean Dip

3 oz (*75 g*) butter beans
2 oz (*50 g*) kidney beans
bouquet garni (bay, parsley, thyme
   and savory)
2 cloves garlic, peeled and chopped
1 tablespoon cold-pressed sunflower
   or safflower oil
1 tablespoon lemon juice
3 tablespoons plain yoghurt
freshly ground black pepper to taste
pinch of salt
freshly grated nutmeg to taste
small spray summer or winter savory
   (about 3 teaspoons of leaves when
   stripped from the stalk)

Herbs: bouquet garni (of bay, parsley, thyme and savory) Extra summer or winter savory (fresh)

This recipe can be made year-round with fresh herbs, using winter savory when summer savory is out of season.

Method   Soak the beans overnight in cold water. Drain, rinse, put into a pan and cover with fresh cold water. Bring to the boil and boil hard for 10 minutes (this is to make sure any harmful enzymes which may be contained in the kidney beans are destroyed).

Add the bouquet garni and garlic and cook for a further 1–1¼ hours (or 20 minutes in a pressure cooker).

Remove the bouquet garni, drain the beans, reserving the liquid. Put them in a liquidizer or food processor with 4 tablespoons of the reserved liquid and the remaining ingredients. Blend to a purée, adding more liquid, if necessary, to achieve a smooth consistency.

(For a more garlicky taste, don't cook the garlic cloves but add them raw at the liquidising stage) (Serves 4–6)

Hummus

4 oz (100 g) dry chick peas
bouquet garni
1 clove garlic OR ½ teaspoon garlic
    granules
juice of ½ lemon
1 tablespoon tahini
freshly ground black pepper
pinch of salt (optional)
¼ pint (150 ml) reserved chick-pea
    liquid
paprika
parsley

Herbs: bouquet garni; parsley to garnish

This is a dish from the Middle East. You *could* use a 15 oz (425 g) can of chick peas to save time, but watch out as most tinned brands have added salt – probably considerably more than the pinch of salt I have allowed, which is in any case optional. Tahini is a paste made from sesame seeds and is available from health food stores.

Method   Soak the chick peas overnight in cold water. Drain, rinse, put in a pan and cover with fresh water. Add the bouquet garni. Bring to the boil, cover the pan tightly and boil hard for 10 minutes.

Reduce the heat and simmer for a further 1–1½ hours until soft, topping up the cooking liquid if necessary. (Or cook for 15 mins in a pressure cooker)

Remove the bouquet garni and drain the chick peas in a colander, reserving the liquid.

Put the peas into a food-processor or liquidizer with the garlic, lemon juice, tahini, pepper and salt and the ¼ pint reserved liquid. Blend to a purée.

Turn into a serving dish, sprinkle with paprika and a little finely snipped fresh parsley. (Serves 4–6)

Sauces and Preserves

Most shop-bought sauces, pickles and chutnies are liberally laced with salt and sugar. But if you make your own, following these specially devised recipes, you can give your meals added interest without a lot of hidden extras.

The Recipes

the herbs to include		*the herbs to include*
1 *Easy Tomato Sauce with Basil*	–	basil
2 *Spiced Tomato Purée Preserve*	–	bouquet garni (parsley, bay, thyme, rosemary)
3 *Yoghurt Cucumber & Mint Relish*	–	mint
4 *'Whitish' Parsley Sauce*	–	parsley
5 *Mint and Apple Chutney*	–	mint
6 *Apricot Lemon Chutney*	–	angelica, lemon balm
7 *Mixed Herb and Vegetable Pickle*	–	rosemary, thyme, hyssop

Easy Tomato Sauce with Basil

1 onion, peeled and finely chopped
1 clove garlic, peeled and crushed
14 oz (397 g) can of tomatoes in natural juice
3 teaspoons fresh or frozen basil
twist of freshly ground black pepper
freshly grated nutmeg

Herb: basil

A simple tomato sauce livens many dishes – and now that it is possible to buy (from larger supermarkets) tinned tomatoes in natural juice, *without* added salt and sugar, it really is amazingly simple to make a quick 'home-made' version that is healthful at the same time.

The tangy taste of basil compensates for the lack of added salt. And don't forget that frozen basil is ideal in cooked recipes when fresh is out of season.

Method Simply put all the ingredients into a heavy-based saucepan and simmer over a low heat, stirring frequently, until reduced to a thick, sauce-like consistency.

For maximum flavour add the basil only in the last few minutes. (Serves 4)

Spiced Tomato Purée Preserve

3 tablespoons olive (or sunflower) oil
4½ lbs (2 k) ripe tomatoes
8 oz (225 g) shallots or onions
bouquet garni (parsley, bay, thyme, rosemary)
2 teaspoons whole mixed pickling spices
3½ fl oz (100 ml) cider vinegar
½ teaspoon salt

Herb: bouquet garni (parsley, bay, thyme, rosemary)

If you grow your own tomatoes and they all seem to be ripe at once, this is an ideal way to preserve them. Shallots give a finer flavour but as they are not always easy to get hold of, ordinary onions will do instead.

The purée will keep for at least a month (or up to a year in the freezer) and can be used to give body and flavour to soups and sauces.

Method Cut the tomatoes into quarters. Peel and cut up the shallots.

Heat the oil in a large, enamelled pan, add the shallots and tomatoes and stir over a fairly high heat for 3–4 minutes. Lower the heat, add the bouquet garni and pickling spices tied in a piece of muslin and simmer until well pulped (about 35 mins).

Remove the herbs and spices. Rub the tomatoes through a fine, non-metal sieve (liquidising doesn't get rid of the pips and skins) return to the pan, add the vinegar and salt and bring to the boil. Boil fast until reduced and thickened (about 15–20 minutes).

Pour into warmed, sterilized jars and seal with non-metal screw-tops or jam-pot covers in the usual way. (Makes about 1 pint (600 ml))

Yoghurt Cucumber and Mint Relish

½ cucumber
5 oz (*125 g*) plain yoghurt
1 tablespoon fresh mint, finely
   chopped OR 3 teaspoons dried
   mint
salt

Herb: mint

I serve this with just about everything, but it is especially good with baked potatoes or a vegetable curry.

It works quite well with dried mint too – provided you dry your own, as commercially dried mint is invariably tasteless and dusty.

Method   Peel, de-seed and dice the cucumber. Put it in a colander, sprinkle with salt and cover with a weighted plate. Leave for 35–40 minutes to drain out excess liquid.

Rinse the cucumber thoroughly to remove the salt, dry in a clean towel, or kitchen paper, then mix it into the yoghurt with the mint. (Serves 3–4)

'Whitish' Parsley Sauce

1 oz (25 g) polyunsaturated margarine
1 oz (25 g) wholemeal flour
½ pint (300 ml) skimmed milk
1 tablespoon chopped parsley
freshly grated nutmeg
freshly ground black pepper
pinch of dry mustard

Herb: parsley (See below for variations)

Based on the traditional white sauce this can be served with vegetables, rice dishes and pasta. The herbs can, of course, be varied accordingly. Try:

> fennel or dill with rice and pasta
> chervil with leeks
> savory with broad beans
> basil with marrow or courgettes

Method   Melt the margarine in a saucepan, add the flour and stir vigorously over a moderately high heat for 2-3 minutes. Remove the pan from the heat and add the milk gradually, stirring continuously.

Bring to the boil, add the herbs and seasoning, then lower the heat so that sauce is just bubbling and cook for a further 3–4 minutes.

(NB Wholemeal flour gives the sauce a delicious nutty flavour but the texture will be less glossy than if white flour were used.)

149

Mint and Apple Chutney

1 lb (450 g) stoned dates
1 lb (450 g) sultanas
1 pint (600 ml) cider vinegar
2 medium cooking apples
2 sweet red apples
1 medium onion, peeled
¾ pint (450 ml) mint leaves – pressed
    down lightly
½ teaspoon salt
½ teaspoon each of coriander
    powder; allspice; clove powder,
    cayenne pepper

Herb: mint

The sweetness in this chutney is provided entirely by the dried fruit and the mint adds an unexpected fresh tang. It is particularly delicious in toasted sandwiches made with curd cheese and served with green salad.

Method Cut up the dates, put them into a large mixing bowl with the sultanas, then pour in the vinegar and leave to stand for several hours until the fruit has softened.

Mince or grate the apples and onion into the bowl, chop the mint finely and add it with the salt and spices. Stir well and leave to stand for 24 hours.

Pot into sterilized jars, seal and label. (Makes about 3½–4 lbs)

Apricot Lemon Chutney

12 oz (325 g) dried apricots
8 oz (225 g) sultanas
1 lb cooking apples, peeled and
  roughly cut up
8 oz (225 g) onions, peeled and
  chopped
1 pint cider vinegar
12 inch (30 cm) stem of angelica, cut
  into small pieces
1 inch (2 cm) cube fresh ginger root,
  grated
bunch of lemon balm leaves, tied
  together
spices (as below) tied in muslin:
  3–4 cloves
  1 teaspoon mustard seed
  1 teaspoon whole pimento
  (allspice)
  1 teaspoon peppercorns
  1 teaspoon coriander seeds

Herbs: angelica, lemon balm

This chutney is softer in texture than the previous uncooked recipe. Angelica provides just the right touch of extra sweetness, as apricots are lower in natural sugar than dates. For a more pronounced lemon flavour add 2–3 teaspoons finely chopped fresh lemon balm to the chutney just before potting.

Method Soak the apricots overnight, drain and put them into a large pan with all the other ingredients. Simmer over a low heat, stirring occasionally, for about 1½ hours until the mixture is thick and pulpy. Remove the spices and lemon balm and pot in sterilised jars in the usual way.

(Makes enough to fill 5 x 1 lb (450 g) jam jars)

Mixed Herb and Vegetable Pickle

1 small cauliflower (½ large one)
8 oz (225 g) pickling onions
1 sweet red pepper
4 oz (100 g) button mushrooms
8 oz (225 g) courgettes or cucumber
8 oz (225 g) firm tomatoes (or green ones if available)
3–4 bay leaves
3–4 small sprigs rosemary
1 sprig hyssop
2 pints (*just over 1 litre*) cider vinegar
1 teaspoon peppercorns
1 teaspoon cloves
1 teaspoon whole pimento
3 inch (*8 cm*) cinnamon stick
1 inch (*2 cm*) cube root ginger peeled and grated
salt for brining

Herbs: rosemary, thyme, hyssop

It is necessary to use salt to extract excess water from the vegetables, so that the vinegar – which acts as a preservative – will not become too diluted. But if you rinse and dry everything well before potting it, the salt content needn't be very high.

Method   First brine the vegetables: Dissolve 1 oz (*25 g*) salt in 1 pint (*600 ml*) water. Divide the cauliflower into florets, peel the onions, cut the pepper into pieces, then put all these into a deep bowl and cover with the salted water. Leave to stand for 24 hours.

Cut the courgettes or cucumber, tomatoes and mushrooms into small neat pieces, put them in a colander and sprinkle with about 1 dessertspoon salt. Stand a weighted plate on top and leave for about 12 hours.

Then prepare the spiced vinegar: Tie the spices in muslin and put them into a pan with the vinegar, bay leaf and a sprig each of rosemary, thyme and hyssop. Bring to boiling point then remove from the heat and leave to stand until cold.

Rinse the vegetables; drain the first set of vegetables, rinse well, then pat dry in a clean towel or kitchen paper. Rinse the second set of vegetables in the colander and pat dry.

Pot and seal: Put a mixture of the prepared vegetables into sterilized jars with a bay leaf and sprig each of rosemary and thyme.

Remove the pickles and herbs from the vinegar and pour enough into each jar to cover the vegetables.

Cover and seal, using jam-pot covers or screw-tops, taking care not to have metal caps in contact with the vinegar.

(Fills 4 x ¾ pint (*450 ml*) capacity jars)

BIBLIOGRAPHY

A discussion paper on proposals for nutritional guidelines for health education in Britain – prepared for the National Advisory Committee on Nutrition Education, otherwise known as the NACNE report – 1983

The Food Scandal   Caroline Walker & Geoffrey Cannon   Century Arrow, 1986

A Modern Herbal   Mrs M. Grieve   Penguin Handbooks, 1980

The Encyclopaedia of Herbs and Herbalism   Malcolm Stuart   Orbis Publishing, 1979

The Herb & Spice Book   Sarah Garland   Francis Lincoln, 1979

The Herb Book   Elizabeth Peplow   W.H. Allen, 1982

Your Very Good Health   Rose Elliott   Fontana, 1981

The Book of Herbs   Dorothy Hall   Pan Books, 1976

Herbs For All Seasons   Rosemary Hemphill   Penguin Books, 1974

INDEX